THE MOST EPIC BASKETBALL STORIES FOR KIDS

Inspiring Young Athletes with Fun and Adventure to Boost Confidence, Mental Toughness, and Team Spirit

W. Bo Cricklewood

INTRODUCTION

The roar of the crowd is deafening. Sweat trickles down your face as you dribble past one defender, then another. The clock's ticking down - 3... 2... 1...

You leap, the ball leaves your fingertips, and time seems to stand still. The arena holds its breath. Then—SWISH! Nothing but net! The crowd erupts! Your teammates rush the court, lifting you onto their shoulders. Confetti rains down, cameras flash, and for a moment, you feel like you're flying. This must be exactly how Michael Jordan felt in Game 6 of the 1998 NBA Finals, when he sank that legendary shot over Bryon Russell, clinching the Bulls' sixth championship. The shot took place with just 5.2

seconds left on the clock, giving the Bulls an 87-86 victory over the Utah Jazz!

But here's the kicker, young baller—that epic moment? It's not just about basketball. It's about life.

Just like MJ's "Last Shot," your journey is full of heart-pounding, palm-sweating, edge-of-your-seat moments. Maybe it's acing that final exam you've been stressing over. Or grabbing the lead role in the school play. Or even mustering up the courage to talk to your crush. Life, like basketball, is a game of moments. It's about seizing opportunities, pushing through challenges, and sometimes, taking that leap of faith when everything's on the line.

Lace up, because we're going to dive into stories that'll make you feel like you're right there on the court with the greatest players who ever hit the court. You'll feel the rush of their triumphs, the sting of their defeats, and most importantly, you'll discover how the lessons they learned on the hardwood can help you become a champion in your own life.

So, are you ready to take the shot? To learn from the best and apply their secrets to your own game—both on and off the court?

Tune out the doubters and get ready for the adventure of a lifetime. Just like in that game-winning moment, anything is possible if you believe in yourself and put in the work. Let's dive in and discover how the spirit of basketball can transform your world.

Now, you might be thinking, "It's just a game, right?" Wrong! Basketball is like that cool teacher who makes learning fun without you even realizing it. It's got more wisdom to share than a library full of textbooks, and the best part? These lessons stick with you long after the final buzzer. Take teamwork, for instance. On the court, five players move as one, like a well-oiled machine. That perfectly timed pass isn't just about padding your assist stats —it's about trust, communication, and having your teammate's back. Sound familiar? That's because these are the same skills that'll help you ace group projects, be a better sibling, or even lead a community project someday. And let's talk about perseverance. In basketball, hitting the floor isn't failure—it's just part of the game. What matters is how fast you jump back up. Every airball, every turnover, every loss—they're not setbacks, they're setups for your comeback. This resilience? It's your ultimate super weapon when life throws you curveballs off the court too.

Discipline is another heavyweight lesson from the hardwood. Those crack-of-dawn practices, the endless drills, the strict training regimes—they're not only about perfecting your jump shot. They're teaching you the value of hard work, dedication, and delayed gratification.

These are the building blocks champions are made of, whether you're aiming for the NBA or dreaming of being the next tech wizard. Time management? Basketball's got you covered. Juggling practices, games, homework, and social life is like running a fast break—you've got to make every second count. It's a skill that'll serve you well when you're balancing college classes or deadlines at your future job.

Leadership isn't just for the captain or the star player. Whether you're calling plays as the point guard or anchoring the defense as center, you're learning to step up, take charge, and inspire others. These are the same qualities that'll help you lead a school club, organize a charity event, or even run a business one day. Ever noticed how the best players keep their cool when the game's on the line? That's emotional control in action, champs! Learning to stay calm under pressure is like gaining a superpower for life's high-stakes moments, be it a job interview one day or a class presentation.

Goal-setting is another life skill you're mastering without even realizing it. Always aiming to improve that free-throw percentage or win the next big game? You're actually learning to set SMART goals, create action plans, and adapt when things don't go as expected. This is the same process that'll help you tackle any big life goal, from acing your SATs to landing your dream job.

And here's a big one—diversity and inclusion. A great basketball team needs all sorts of players with different strengths. You're learning to appreciate various skills, work with all kinds of people, and create an environment where everyone can shine. In today's global world, this understanding is worth its weight in gold.

In the chapters ahead, you're about to meet some of the most incredible ballers to ever grace the hardwood. We're talking legends who revolutionized the game, underdogs who defied the odds, and modern-day heroes who are rewriting the record books as we speak. But we're not just going to show you their highlight reels. We're taking you behind the scenes—to the blood, sweat, and tears behind the victory, the sting of defeat, and the sweet taste of redemption. You'll walk in their shoes, from the neighborhood courts where they first fell in love with the game to the roaring arenas where they became legends.

These aren't just basketball stories—they're life stories. Tales of overcoming adversity, chasing dreams, and becoming the best version of yourself.

As you read, you might start to see yourself in these stories. You'll see that these basketball greats started out just like you—with doubts, fears, and obstacles. But they persevered, believed in themselves, and changed their lives—and sometimes the world—through basketball.

You'll meet players who rose from humble beginnings to become stars, not just through their skills on the court, but through grit, smart choices, and an unbreakable spirit. You'll read about coaches who spotted potential in unexpected places and nurtured it into greatness. You'll discover teams that came together to achieve the impossible, showing what true unity and determination can accomplish.

These stories might pop into your head when you're stuck on a tough homework problem, when you're nervous about auditioning for the school play, or when you're thinking about giving up on a big dream. They'll remind you that if they pushed through, so can you.

But don't worry—this book isn't all serious business. We've got some hilarious locker room tales, jaw-dropping trick shots, and behind-the-scenes shenanigans that'll have you in stitches. Because at its heart, basketball (and life) is about having fun, and that's exactly what we're here to do!

Here's how the book is laid out:

We've got chapters focusing on different aspects of basketball and life. Each chapter features two amazing stories that'll leave you inspired.

But we don't stop there. After each pair of stories, there's a special section diving into the Big Lesson. We connect the dots between what you've read and your own life, showing how these lessons apply both on and off the court.

Imagine reading about how Michael Jordan turned the disappointment of being cut from his high school team into the fuel that drove him to become the GOAT. In the lesson section, we explore how setbacks can be the setup for incredible comebacks—in sports and in life.

These basketball stories are invitations to see yourself and the world in a whole new way. To uncover strengths you never knew you had. To dream bigger than you ever thought possible.

So, are you ready? Ready to laugh, learn, and be inspired? Ready to see the game of basketball—and yourself—through fresh eyes?

Take a deep breath. Feel the texture of the ball in your hands. Listen to the squeak of sneakers on the court. Breathe in that mix of excitement and determination in the air.

Now, square up. Plant your feet. Keep your eyes on the target. This is your moment. Your shot at seeing how the lessons from the court can change your game—in basketball and in life. The clock's ticking. The crowd's on its feet. Everything you've experienced, everything you are, comes down to this moment.

Are you ready to take your shot? It's going to be nothing but net!

CHAPTER 1:

Overcoming Adversity

Alright, hoop dreamers and future MVPs! This isn't just about nailing that tricky crossover or perfecting your jump shot. Nope, we're talking about facing life's full-court press and coming out on top!

So, imagine you're down by 20 in the fourth quarter. The crowd's against you, your shots aren't falling, and it feels like the basketball gods have turned their backs.

What do you do? Throw in the towel?

No way! This is where the real ballers shine, and guess what? Life's got a whole lot of fourth quarters waiting for you.

Adversity—a fancy word for "when things get tough," and let me tell you, things get tough for everyone—even the superstars whose posters are plastered on your bedroom walls. We're talking about injuries that make you wince, financial struggles that would make your piggy bank cry, and personal setbacks that feel like face-planting in the playground. But, it's not about avoiding these challenges. It's about how you bounce back when life tries to swat your shot.

Do you think adversity is just for us regular folks?

Think again! Every hoops legend you've ever heard of has had to stare down their own personal adversity. Michael Jordan didn't make his high school varsity team on the first try. Steph Curry was told he was too small for the NBA. The list goes on and on. But you know what? They didn't let those setbacks define them. Instead, they used them as fuel to light a fire under their dreams. Here's the cool part: overcoming these obstacles isn't just about becoming a better baller. It's about leveling up in the game of life. Every time you face a challenge head-on, you're building your character, toughening your mental game, and developing the kind of resilience that will serve you whether you're on the court or in the classroom.

Remember that time you thought you'd never understand algebra? Or when you were sure you'd mess up your piano recital? But you put in the work, gritted your teeth, and came out on top? That's the same spirit that turns good players into legends. It's not about never falling down—it's about how quickly you get back up, dust yourself off, and get back in the game.

Now, get ready to meet two absolute legends of the basketball world who know a thing or two about facing adversity: Derrick Rose and LeBron James. These guys aren't only masters of the hardwood; they're Ph.D. holders in the School of Hard Knocks.

Derrick Rose? This dude was the youngest MVP in NBA history. And then there's LeBron James. Yeah, yeah, I know what you're thinking. "King James? What adversity did he face?" Well, young LeBron's story isn't all championship rings and MVP trophies. These two ballers faced totally different challenges. But both of them? They showed us that it's not about what knocks you down —it's about how you respond when you're on the mat.

As we dive into their stories, I want you to put yourself in their sneakers. Maybe you're not facing NBA-level pressure, but I bet you've got your own challenges. That homework that seems impossible? That friend drama that's got you stressed? The family stuff that keeps you up at night? That's your adversity, your fourth-quarter deficit.

But here's the thing—you're not alone in this game.

So, are you ready to learn from the best? To see how true champions face their fears, overcome their doubts, and rise above their circumstances? To discover how you can apply their strategies to your own life and become the MVP of your own story?

Of course, you are! Because on the other side of every challenge is a stronger, smarter, more resilient you.

Derrick Rose: Overcoming Multiple Injuries

Let's step back into one of the most epic comeback stories in NBA history. We're talking about none other than Derrick Rose, the man who stared career-ending injuries in the face and said, "Not today!"

It's 2011, and a 22-year-old D-Rose is setting the basketball world on total fire. This Chicago kid, straight outta the South Side, becomes the youngest MVP in NBA history. Let that sink in for a second. Youngest. MVP. Ever! He's got the speed of a cheetah, the hops of a kangaroo, and the court vision of an eagle. The future's so bright, he's gotta wear shades, right?

But then, BOOM! Life throws a curveball that would make even the toughest players crumble.

It's April 28, 2012. The Bulls are cruising in Game 1 of the playoffs. Rose goes up for a layup—something he's done a million times before. But this time, when he lands, everything changes. His left knee buckles. The entire arena goes silent. You could hear a basketball drop. Diagnosis? Torn ACL! The Anterior Cruciate Ligament is a key ligament in the knee that helps stabilize the joint. It's important for movements like pivoting, cutting, and sudden stops, which are common in sports. For those of you who don't speak "sports injury," that's like telling a cheetah it can't run anymore. Most players would be devastated. Some might even call it quits. But D-Rose? He's built differently.

Rose attacks his rehab like it's Game 7 of the Finals. He's in the gym when others are sleeping. He's working on his game when others are on vacation. But just when he's about to return— WHAM! Another setback. This time it's his right knee. Torn meniscus (a C-shaped piece of cartilage in the knee that acts as a cushion between the thighbone and shinbone, helping to absorb shock and stabilize the joint). Are you kidding me?

Now, let's be real for a second. How many of you would keep going after that? It's like studying super hard for a test, and then getting sick on exam day. Then, when you're finally better and ready to take the makeup test, you break your writing hand. It's enough to make anyone want to give up.

But giving up? That's not in Rose's vocabulary.

Here's where it gets really inspiring. Rose doesn't just work on healing his body. He works on strengthening his mind. He's not just rehabbing his knees; he's rebuilding his whole approach to the game. It's like when you're struggling with a subject in school, and instead of just memorizing facts, you learn how to learn. Rose is relearning basketball, but this time with the wisdom that comes from facing adversity.

But what about his incredible athleticism? His speed? His insane vertical leap? Well, here's the cool part. Rose doesn't try to be the same player he was before. Instead, he evolves. He adapts. It's like a video game character who loses some speed points but gains in wisdom and strategy. The new D-Rose might not be soaring for highlight-reel dunks every night, but he's craftier. His court vision? Sharper than ever. His mid-range game? Smooth as butter. He's like a basketball Jedi, using the force (or in this case, his basketball IQ) more than raw physical power.

But let's not sugarcoat it. This comeback? It wasn't all swishes and alley-oops. Rose faced doubters. People said he was washed up, and that he should retire. Some fans turned their backs on him. Imagine working your butt off to come back from an injury, only to have people tell you to quit. That's the kind of mental pressure that could break even the toughest players.

But Rose? He's got mental armor stronger than vibranium (yeah, I just dropped a Black Panther reference). Every doubt, every criticism, every setback—he uses them all as fuel. It's like he's got a little voice in his head saying, "Prove them wrong, Derrick. Prove. Them. Wrong."

And boy, does he ever.

Fast forward to 2018. Rose drops 50 points in a game against the Utah Jazz.

Fifty. Points!

After everything he's been through. The crowd goes wild. His teammates are in tears. Even opponents are cheering for him. It's like watching a real-life sports movie, but better, because it's real. That 50-point game? It's awesome, but it's not even the best part of Rose's story. The best part is every single day he chose to keep going. Every morning he woke up and said, "I'm not done yet." Every time he stepped on the court, whether he scored 2 points or 20, he was winning his personal battle.

So, what can we learn from D-Rose?

- First off, setbacks don't define you. They refine you. Rose could have let his injuries be the end of his story. Instead, he made them the beginning of a new chapter. Think about that the next time you face a setback. Failed a test? Didn't make the team? Got rejected by your crush? That's not the end. It's just the start of your comeback story.

- Second, adaptability is a superpower. Rose couldn't be the same player he was before, so he became a new, arguably better version of himself. In a world that's always changing, being able to adapt is like having a cheat code for life.

- Third, mental toughness is just as important as physical strength. Maybe even more so. Rose's body might have been broken, but his spirit? Unbreakable. That's the kind of toughness that doesn't just win games - it wins at life.

- And finally, never, ever give up on your dreams. Rose could have walked away from basketball. He had money, fame, and an MVP trophy. But he loved the game too much to quit. What do you love that much? What dream would you fight for, even when everything seems stacked against you?

Derrick Rose's story isn't just about basketball. It's about facing your fears, overcoming obstacles, and writing your own destiny. It's about falling down seven times and getting up eight. It's about looking adversity in the eye and saying, "You can't stop me."

So the next time you're facing your own personal injury—whether it's a bad grade, a tough break-up, or just a day when nothing seems to go right—remember D-Rose. Remember the kid from Chicago who refused to let injuries steal his dream.

Remember that comebacks are always possible, that adaptability is key, and that the strength of your mind can overcome the limits of your body.

LeBron James: Rising from Disadvantage

Picture Akron, Ohio, in the 1990s. It's not exactly the land of milk and honey. And right in the middle of this tough town is a little kid named LeBron. Now, LeBron's early life? It's like playing a game with the difficulty set to "Extreme."

No stable home? Check. LeBron and his mom, Gloria, moved more times than he could count. We're talking 12 times in 3 years! Imagine trying to make friends or keep up with school when you're bouncing around like a basketball. Poverty? Oh yeah. There were days when LeBron didn't know where his next meal was coming from. Absent father? Yep. LeBron's dad wasn't in the picture, leaving Gloria to play both Mom and Dad.

But here's where it gets interesting. Instead of letting these challenges crush him, young LeBron found an escape. And that escape? A round, orange ball and a hoop.

Basketball became more than a game for LeBron. It was his lifeline, his ticket to a better future. When life was chaotic, the basketball court was where things made sense. When the real world was tough, LeBron could create his own world between those baselines. On the court, it didn't matter if his clothes were secondhand. It didn't matter if he didn't know where he'd be sleeping that night. All that mattered was the ball, the hoop, and his growing skills.

And boy, did those skills grow! LeBron wasn't just good—he was scary good. Like, "Is this kid even human?" good. By high school, he wasn't just playing the game; he was rewriting it. LeBron's high school games were on national TV. His jerseys were selling out before he even went pro. He was on the cover of

Sports Illustrated as a junior, dubbed "The Chosen One." Talk about pressure! But LeBron? He thrived on it.

Then came the NBA draft in 2003. Imagine the whole basketball world holding its breath, waiting to see where this kid from Akron would land. And boom! First pick overall to his hometown team, the Cleveland Cavaliers. It was like a movie script come to life! But here's the really cool part. As LeBron's star rose, he didn't forget where he came from. Nope, he looked at his success and thought, "How can I use this to help kids like me?"

- He started the LeBron James Family Foundation, pouring millions into education and community programs in Akron.

- He opened the I Promise School, giving kids from tough backgrounds a chance at a great education.

- He's provided scholarships, mentoring programs, and even housing for families in need.

LeBron didn't only climb out of disadvantage—he built an elevator to bring others up with him. How's that for a real-life superhero?

Remember, your circumstances don't define you—your response to them does. LeBron could have let his tough childhood beat him down. Instead, he used it as rocket fuel to launch himself— and others—to new heights.

So, next time you're facing a tough situation, channel your inner LeBron.

Lesson: Mental Resilience and Perseverance

Now is the perfect time to hit the mental gym! We've seen how Derrick Rose and LeBron James faced their challenges head-on and came out on top. Now, let's break down the secret that made it all possible: mental resilience and perseverance.

First up, what exactly are we talking about here?

- **Mental resilience:** Think of this as your mind's ability to bounce back from setbacks. It's like having a trampoline in your brain—the harder life pushes you down, the higher you bounce back up!

- **Perseverance:** This is your "never give up" muscle. It's what keeps you going when things get tough and when everyone else has thrown in the towel.

How did our basketball heroes show these superpowers?

Derrick Rose:

- **Mental resilience:** Every time an injury tried to end his career, Rose's mind said, "Nice try, but I'm not done yet." He didn't just heal his body; he strengthened his mind.

- **Perseverance:** Rose kept coming back, again and again. He reinvented his game, adapted his style, and proved the doubters wrong. That's perseverance with a capital P!

LeBron James:

- **Mental resilience:** LeBron could have let his tough childhood define him. Instead, he used it as motivation to build a better future.

- **Perseverance:** From practicing for hours on end as a kid to continuously improving his game as a pro, LeBron's work ethic is legendary. He never stops pushing to be better.

Level Up

So, how can you build your own mental resilience and perseverance? Here are some strategies straight from the playbook of champions:

- **Embrace the Growth Mindset:**

  - **See challenges as opportunities to grow, not obstacles to avoid:** When you face something tough, like a hard math problem or a challenging basketball move, think of it as a chance to learn and get better. Instead of saying, "I can't do this," try saying, "This is a chance for me to improve!"

  - **Tell yourself, "I can't do it... yet." That little word "yet" is powerful!** Adding "yet" to the end of your thoughts can change how you see your abilities. It means you might not be able to do something now, but with practice and effort, you will get there.

- **Set SMART Goals: Break Those Big Dreams Into Smaller, Manageable Steps:**

  - **Specific:** Your goal should be clear and detailed, like a treasure map that shows exactly where to go. Instead of saying "I want to be a better basketball player," be specific about what you want to improve.

    - **How to apply it:** Decide what part of basketball you want to get better at. For example, "I want to improve my shooting skills, so I can make more baskets during games."

- **Example:** Instead of a vague goal, say: "I want to practice shooting free throws to make at least 8 out of 10 shots."

o **Measurable:** Your goal should have a way to track your progress, like counting the number of times you hit a target.

- **How to apply it:** You need to measure how well you're doing to know if you're improving.

- **Example:** You can use a notebook or a phone app to record how many free throws you make out of 10 attempts each day. You'll keep track of your scores over time to see if you're getting better.

o **Achievable:** Your goal should be something you can realistically reach, given your current skills and resources. It shouldn't be too easy or too hard.

- **How to apply it:** Make sure your goal is realistic based on your current skill level and how much time you can spend practicing.

- **Example:** If you're currently making only 3 out of 10 free throws, aiming to make 8 out of 10 is challenging but possible with practice. Ensure you have access to a basketball hoop and time to practice regularly.

○ **Relevant:** Your goal should matter to you and fit with what you really want to achieve in basketball. It should be important to your overall goal.

  ▪ **How to apply it:** Make sure improving your shooting helps with your bigger goal in basketball, like playing well in games or making the team.

  ▪ **Example:** Practicing free throws is relevant because making more baskets will help you score more points during games and be a better player overall.

○ **Time-bound:** Your goal should have a deadline or a time frame, like setting a date for a party. This helps you stay on track and motivated.

  ▪ **How to apply it:** Decide when you want to achieve your goal and set a deadline to help you focus your practice.

  ▪ **Example:** Set a goal to make 8 out of 10 free throws by the end of the month. This gives you a specific time frame to work towards.

- **Practice Positive Self-Talk:**

○ Be your own cheerleader. What would you say to encourage a friend? Say that to yourself! When you're feeling down or doubting yourself, imagine what a friend would say to cheer you up and say those things to yourself. For example, tell yourself, "You've got this!" instead of "I'm not good enough."

○ Replace "I can't" with "I'll try" or "I'm working on it." Instead of saying, "I can't do this," say, "I'll give it my best shot" or "I'm practicing to get better." This helps you stay positive and focused on improvement.

- **Learn from Failure:**

  o Ask yourself, "What can I learn from this?" after setbacks: When something doesn't go as planned, like missing a goal or getting a low grade, think about what you can learn from the experience. It's not about feeling bad; it's about figuring out what you can do better next time.

  o Remember, failure is not the opposite of success – it's part of success! Failing is just one step on the road to success. Each time you fail, you learn something new, and that helps you get closer to achieving your goals.

- **Build a Support System:**

  o Surround yourself with people who believe in you: Spend time with friends, family, and mentors who encourage you and support your dreams. Having people who believe in you makes it easier to stay motivated and work towards your goals.

  o Don't be afraid to ask for help when you need it: If you're struggling with something, like a difficult homework problem or a tricky basketball skill, it's okay to ask for help. Reaching out for support shows strength and helps you find solutions faster.

- **Develop a Routine:**

  o Create habits that support your goals: Set up a regular schedule for practicing your skills or working on your homework. Doing small, consistent actions every day helps you make steady progress toward your goals.

- ○ Consistency is key–small actions every day add up to big results: Even if you practice a little bit each day, those small efforts will build up over time. Just like brushing your teeth every day keeps them clean, regular practice helps you improve steadily.

- **Visualize Success:**

- ○ Picture yourself overcoming challenges and achieving your goals: Imagine yourself succeeding, like making a winning shot in basketball or finishing a tough project. This mental practice can help you feel more confident and prepared for real-life challenges.

- ○ Your mind doesn't know the difference between vivid imagination and reality–use this to your advantage! By vividly imagining your success, you can trick your brain into believing that you're capable of achieving your goals, which can boost your confidence and motivation.

- **Practice Mindfulness:**

- ○ Stay present in the moment: Focus on what you're doing right now, whether it's studying, playing sports, or talking with friends. Being present helps you stay focused and enjoy each moment.

- ○ Learn to observe your thoughts without judgment: Notice what you're thinking without criticizing yourself. If you're worried or frustrated, just recognize those feelings and let them pass, without letting them control how you feel or act.

IRL (In Real Life)

Let's bring this off the court and into your world. How can you apply these lessons to the challenges you might face?

- **In School:**
  - **Tough class:** Channel your inner D-Rose. If you're struggling in a subject, don't give up. Adapt your study strategy, seek help, and keep pushing. Remember, Rose didn't just rehab his body—he reshaped his entire game.

  - **Big project:** Think like LeBron. Break it down into smaller tasks, set deadlines for each part, and tackle them one by one. Just like LeBron didn't become a superstar overnight, you'll build your project step by step.

- **In Sports:**
  - **Not making the team:** Use the LeBron mindset. Instead of getting discouraged, use it as motivation to work harder. Set specific goals to improve your skills, and don't let temporary setbacks stop you.

  - **Performance slump:** Take a page from Rose's book. Analyze what's not working, be willing to change your approach, and keep showing up. Remember, Rose's comeback wasn't just about healing—it was about reinvention.

- **In Personal Life:**
  - **Friend drama:** Apply the mental resilience you've learned. Step back, take a breath, and look for constructive

solutions. Remember, both Rose and LeBron faced criticism and doubters—it's how you respond that matters.

- ○ **Family challenges:** Channel LeBron's spirit of giving back. If things are tough at home, look for ways you can contribute positively, even if it's just by maintaining a good attitude or helping out more.

Now, it's your turn to reflect. Think about a time when you faced adversity:

- What was the challenge?
- How did you respond?
- Looking back, how could you have applied the lessons from Rose and James?
- How can you use what you've learned for future challenges?

Remember, every great story has obstacles. It's how the hero overcomes them that makes the story worth telling. Rose and James aren't only basketball legends because of their physical skills—it was their mental game that set them apart.

So, the next time life tries to swat your shot:

- Be like Rose—adapt, evolve, and never stop believing in yourself.
- Be like LeBron—use your challenges as fuel and remember to lift others as you rise.

Your mind is your most powerful muscle. Train it, trust it, and watch how it transforms not just your game, but your entire life.

You've got the ball now. What's your next move going to be?

CHAPTER 2:

The Importance of Practice

It's 5 AM and the world's still snoozing, but you? You're already on the court, the rhythmic bounce of the ball echoing in the empty gym. Swish after swish, drill after drill. Sound familiar? No? Well, it should, because that's the secret of every basketball legend you've ever heard of!

Are you thinking: "Practice? Come on, that's boring! I want to be in the game, hitting game-winners, hearing the crowd roar!" Sure. We all want to be the hero, the one who hits that buzzer-beater in Game 7 of the Finals. But here's the thing—those magical moments? They're built on a foundation of thousands of hours of practice when no one's watching. Let's break it down.

Practice isn't just about shooting hoops until your arms feel like noodles (although that's part of it). It's a full-on mind and body workout. It's about:

- **Muscle memory:** Ever wonder how Steph Curry can sink those ridiculous 3-pointers without even looking at the basket? That's muscle memory, baby! It's like teaching your body to play basketball on autopilot.

- **Mental toughness:** You're familiar with this one. Practice is where you build that iron will. It's where you push through when your legs are burning, your lungs are screaming, and that little voice in your head is begging you to quit.

- **Skill refinement:** This is where you turn those clumsy dribbles into silky smooth handles, where airballs become nothing-but-net swishes.

- **Confidence boosting:** Nothing, and I mean nothing, builds confidence like knowing you've put in the work. When you step on that court for game time, you're not hoping to play well—you know you will.

But here's the real kicker—practice isn't just about basketball. The lessons you learn on the court? They're life lessons, my friends. That dedication, that drive to improve, that ability to push through when things get tough? That's the stuff that turns good players into legends, and regular kids into world-changers.

"But I'm not a natural athlete. What's the point?"

Hold up right there! Even the most gifted ballers in history relied on practice to reach the top. Michael Jordan? Remember, he was cut from his high school team. But he practiced like a maniac and became, well, Michael Jordan! Natural talent is great, but it's practice that turns potential into greatness. And it's not about practicing 24/7. It's about smart practice. Quality over quantity, folks. One focused hour can be worth more than five distracted ones. It's about being present, being intentional, and always, always pushing to be better than you were yesterday.

In this chapter, we're going to look at two absolute practice monsters: Kobe Bryant and Stephen Curry. These guys didn't just practice—they revolutionized practice. They took it to a whole new level. Kobe's "Mamba Mentality" wasn't just a catchy phrase —it was a way of life. And Curry? He turned practice into an art form, developing drills so innovative they changed the game of basketball itself. These players didn't just go through the motions. They didn't just show up. They attacked practice with the same intensity they brought to Game 7 of the NBA Finals. And the results? Well, the banners hanging in the rafters and the rings on their fingers speak for themselves.

I want you to think about your own practice routine. Are you just going through the motions, or are you attacking each session like it's your last? Are you pushing your limits, or staying comfortable? Are you practicing to participate, or practicing to dominate?

Remember, every time you step on that court to practice, you're not just working on your jump shot or your dribbling. You're laying the foundation for your dreams.

Kobe Bryant—The "Mamba Mentality" and Intense Training

Hoop dreamers, strap in because we're diving straight into the mind of one of the most intense, dedicated, and flat-out legendary players to ever grace the hardwood—Kobe Bryant. The Black Mamba. The embodiment of the phrase "hard work beats talent when talent doesn't work hard."

Kobe's approach to practice wasn't just next level—it was next universe. This guy didn't just embrace the grind; he redefined it. Welcome to the world of "Mamba Mentality." So, what exactly is this "Mamba Mentality" we keep hearing about? In Kobe's own words, it means "to constantly try to be the best version of yourself." Sounds simple, right? But the way Kobe lived it was anything but.

The clock strikes at a solid 4:15 AM. The world's still deep in dreamland. But Kobe? He's already at the gym, ready to start his first workout of the day. That's right, first. As in, there's more to come. A lot more.

Kobe's typical day looked something like this:

- 4:15 AM - 7:00 AM: First workout (conditioning, strength training)
- 7:00 AM - 11:00 AM: Breakfast and family time
- 11:00 AM - 4:00 PM: Basketball skills training

- 4:00 PM - 6:00 PM: Weight training and conditioning

- 7:00 PM - 11:00 PM: More skills training

That's not a typo! We're talking about 6-7 hours of training every single day. And not just during the season—this was year-round. While other players were lounging on beaches during the off-season, Kobe was in the gym, perfecting his craft. But it wasn't just about the hours. It was about the intensity. Kobe approached every practice like it was Game 7 of the NBA Finals. He once said, "I can't remember the last time I was tired." Why? Because he had trained his body and mind to push past exhaustion. Kobe Bryant's "666" workout was an intense training routine where he dedicated 6 hours a day, 6 days a week, for 6 months. This grueling regimen included conditioning, strength training, and basketball drills, designed to push his body and mind to the limit. It shows just how committed Kobe was to becoming one of the best players ever, proving that hard work and persistence pay off big time.

Here are some of Kobe's legendary practice habits:

- The 400-shot rule: Every single day, no matter what, Kobe would make 400 shots. Not take 400 shots—make them. Even on game days. Even on Christmas.

- First to arrive, last to leave: Kobe was notorious for being the first player at practice and the last to leave. He'd often be practicing alone in the dark after everyone else had gone home.

- Obsessive skill repetition: Kobe would fixate on perfecting a single move, practicing it hundreds, even thousands of times until it was flawless.

- Studying film: Kobe wasn't just physically preparing; he was mentally sharpening his game by studying hours of game footage, both of himself and his opponents.

- Creating weaknesses: Kobe would intentionally practice with a weighted vest or workout in high-altitude conditions to challenge himself further.

The results? Five NBA championships. Two Olympic gold medals. 18 All-Star selections. And a legacy that will inspire generations of players to come.

But Kobe's impact went far beyond his personal achievements. His work ethic became legendary, inspiring not just basketball players, but athletes across all sports and even people outside of sports entirely. Stories of Kobe's insane work ethic spread like wildfire. There's the tale of him practicing for hours in the dark when the lights went out in the gym. Or the time he challenged his high school teammates to a one-on-one tournament... while on crutches. Or how he'd practice without a ball, just going through the motions of his shots over and over again.

These stories didn't just impress people—they changed the game. A whole generation of players grew up wanting to "be like Kobe," not just in terms of skill, but in terms of work ethic. Players like Kyrie Irving, Devin Booker, and Jayson Tatum have all spoken about how Kobe's approach to practice influenced their own. But here's the really cool part—Kobe's influence wasn't limited to superstars. His "Mamba Mentality" resonated with people from all walks of life. Students pulling all-nighters for exams, entrepreneurs working tirelessly on their startups, and artists perfecting their craft—all found inspiration in Kobe's relentless pursuit of excellence.

Kobe showed us that greatness isn't born—it's built, one grueling practice session at a time. He proved that with enough dedication, enough passion, and yes, enough practice, you can achieve things that others might consider impossible.

So, the next time you're tempted to skip practice, or take it easy, or "just get by," remember the Mamba. Remember the countless hours he put in when no one was watching. Remember the sacrifices he made, the pain he pushed through, the limits he shattered.

Ask yourself: Are you practicing to be good, or are you practicing to be great? Are you pushing your limits, or staying in your comfort zone? Are you embracing the Mamba Mentality?

Because here's the truth: You might not have Kobe's natural talents. You might not have his physical gifts. But his work ethic? His dedication? His relentless drive to improve? That's available to every single one of you. That's a choice you can make every single day.

So, what's it going to be? Are you ready to embrace your inner Mamba?

Remember, as Kobe himself said, "Great things come from hard work and perseverance. No excuses."

Now get out there and make the Mamba proud!

Stephen Curry—From Underrated Prospect to Superstar

Yup, we're gonna be talking about Stephen Curry—the guy who turned the basketball world upside down and inside out!

It's 2006, and high school senior Steph is out there breaking ankles and swishing shots like it's nobody's business. But here's the kicker—nobody's buying what he's selling! Can you believe it? This future NBA superstar was getting passed over like last week's cafeteria mystery meat!

Why? 'Cause Steph was about as beefy as a stringbean! At 6 feet tall and barely tipping the scales at 160 pounds soaking wet, scouts were giving him the cold shoulder. "Too small," they said. "Too weak," they grumbled. But you know what Steph heard? "Challenge accepted, baby!" While other kids were busy leveling up in video games, Steph was leveling up in real life! He turned the gym into his second home. But we're not talking about your average, run-of-the-mill practice sessions. Nuh-uh! Steph was cooking up some next-level, out-of-this-world training that would make even pro ballers do a double-take!

Check this out: Steph didn't just practice shooting—he turned it into a full-blown art form! He'd spend hours, and I mean HOURS, shooting from every single spot on the court. Close-range, mid-range, long-range, you name it! But here's where Steph went full-on basketball mad scientist: he started launching shots from way beyond the arc. We're talking shots that would make most coaches lose their minds faster than a ref's whistle!

Fun Fact Alert! Did you know Steph wouldn't wrap up his practice until he drained 500 shots? Not 500 attempts, 500

MAKES! That's like scoring 125 points in a real game! By the time most of us would be ready to throw in the towel, Steph was just getting warmed up!

But hold onto your headbands, 'cause we're just getting started! Steph knew that to really shine, he needed to handle the rock like it was an extension of his arm. So, he cooked up some of the craziest dribbling drills you've ever seen. We're talking two-ball dribbling while wearing special goggles that block his lower vision. Yeah, you heard that right! Steph would be out there looking like a basketball-dribbling spaceman, training his hands to move without his eyes watching them. Talk about next-level dedication! Here's another nugget of Curry craziness for ya: Steph would practice his ball-handling skills with a tennis ball! Why? Because if you can control a tiny tennis ball, a basketball feels like a beach ball in comparison. This drill helped Steph develop those lightning-quick hands that leave defenders scratching their heads!

Now, let's fast forward a bit. All that blood, sweat, and probably a few tears (hey, even future MVPs have tough days) paid off big time! That scrawny kid nobody wanted? He's now the guy that makes even the toughest defenders wake up in a cold sweat! Steph didn't just join the NBA—he flipped the script and rewrote the whole playbook!

Get this: Before Curry came along, taking a three-pointer was like rolling the dice. Now? It's hotter than a fresh batch of nachos at halftime! Steph's sharpshooting ways have changed the entire landscape of basketball. Teams are scrambling to find players who can shoot like Steph (spoiler alert: good luck with that!). But here's the real kicker—Steph didn't just stop once he made it to the big leagues. Nope, he doubled down harder than a blackjack player with pocket aces! Even as an NBA superstar, with all the fame and bling, Steph still practices like he's that underdog kid with something to prove.

Wanna know how serious Steph is about his craft? During his MVP seasons, he'd still show up hours before game time to go through his insane shooting routine. We're talking about a guy who once made 77 straight 3-pointers in practice! That's not a typo—seventy-seven in a row! Most of us can't even make 77 free throws in a row, and this guy's doing it from downtown!

So, what's the secret to Steph's success story?

It wasn't some magical growth spurt or a slam-dunk gift from the basketball gods. Nope, it was good old-fashioned hard work, with a side of never-say-die attitude. It was thousands of hours in the gym when nobody was watching, perfecting his craft like a basketball Picasso.

Here's the slam dunk truth: Steph Curry's journey isn't just about basketball. It's a masterclass in chasing your dreams, no matter how many people try to bench your ambitions. It's about believing in yourself when the whole world's telling you to sit down and shut up. It's about practicing not just until you get it right, but until you can't get it wrong.

So, the court's calling. The ball's in your hands. Are you ready to put in the work and change the game? Remember, every great player, every basketball legend, started exactly where you are right now. The only difference? They never stopped practicing, never stopped improving, never stopped believing.

Lesson—Dedication and Consistent Effort

We've talked about the jaw-dropping journeys of some serious basketball legends. But now it's time to get real. What's the epic secret that turned these ordinary kids into extraordinary players? Two words: dedication and consistent effort.

"Dedication? Consistent effort? Sounds like something my parents would say!"

But hang with me here, because this isn't just some boring lecture. This is the key to unlocking your full potential—not just in basketball, but in anything you set your mind to.

So what exactly do we mean by dedication and consistent effort? Well, imagine you're playing your favorite video game. You know, the one where you're trying to beat that impossible level. You try once, twice, a hundred times. You're frustrated, your thumbs are sore, but you keep going. Why? Because you're dedicated to beating that level. You put in consistent effort, trying new strategies, learning from your mistakes, until finally—victory!

That feeling of triumph? That's what dedication and consistent effort are all about.

Now, let's bring it back to the court.

Remember Steph Curry's insane practice routines? That's dedication in action. When everyone else was calling it a day, Steph was still in the gym, shooting hundreds of three-pointers. And he didn't just do it once in a while when he felt like it. Nope, he did it day after day, week after week, year after year. That's consistent effort.

But here's the thing—dedication and consistent effort aren't just about putting in long hours. It's about making those hours count. It's about practicing with purpose, always pushing yourself to get better. Think about it like this: if you're spending an hour practicing your shot, but you're just lazily throwing up bricks, are you getting better? Probably not. But, if you're locked in—focusing on your form, your release, your follow-through—now you're cooking with gas. This kind of intentional practice is the rocket fuel that launches players from good to unstoppable.

Now, I get it. We're not all going to be the next Steph Curry or Kobe Bryant. But that's not the point. The point is that we can all apply these lessons to our own lives, whether we're trying to make the school basketball team or ace our next math test.

Let's break it down into some strategies you can use to level up your own practice game:

- **Set specific goals:** Forget vague goals like "I want to be better." How about "I'll raise my free throw percentage by 10% this month"? Boom. Now you've got a target, and every practice session has a purpose.

- **Create a schedule:** Rain or shine, lock in that practice time. Decide when and how long you'll train. Whether it's 30 minutes or two hours, consistency builds champions.

- **Focus on quality, not just quantity:** It's not about how many hours you practice, but how you use those hours. Zone in, block out the noise, and make every minute count in whatever it is that you're busy with. Be present, be in the moment. You learn from your past to make changes in the present in order to build a better future.

- **Track your progress:** Keep a log of your practice sessions and your improvements. Seeing your progress can be a huge motivator!

- **Embrace the grind:** Not every practice session will be fun. There will be days when you're tired, frustrated, or just not feeling it. Push through those days—that's where real growth happens.

- **Learn from your mistakes:** Don't get discouraged when you mess up. Instead, analyze what went wrong and how you can do better next time.

- **Celebrate small wins:** Did you make 10 free throws in a row for the first time? Awesome! Acknowledge these small victories—they add up to big improvements over time.

- **Find your flow:** You know that feeling when you're totally in the zone? That's flow. To get there, challenge yourself just enough so that you're fully engaged, but not frustrated. When you hit that sweet spot, time flies, and you'll practice better without even noticing.

- **Mix it up:** Don't just stick to one drill or method. Variety not only makes practice less boring but also trains different parts of your game. Maybe today it's shooting drills, tomorrow it's defensive work. Keeping things fresh helps your overall growth and prevents burnout.

- **Visualize your success:** Top athletes use visualization techniques to mentally rehearse their moves before they hit the court. Try it out—imagine yourself sinking that free throw or acing that test. Your brain can't always tell the difference between real and imagined practice, so it's like extra training time.

- **Surround yourself with people who push you:** You're only as good as the people around you. If your friends or teammates push you to improve, you'll level up even faster. Friendly competition and support from your crew help you stay motivated and keep striving for more.

- **Rest is part of the grind:** Rest is as crucial as the hard work. Without proper recovery, you won't make gains, and burnout becomes real. Prioritize sleep, stretching, and days off to let your body and mind reset so you can come back stronger.

These strategies don't just apply to basketball. You can use them for anything you want to improve at. Let's say you're struggling with algebra. Could you set a goal to solve 10 extra problems each day? Could you create a study schedule and stick to it? Could you track your test scores to see your progress? You bet!

Or maybe you're learning to play guitar. Could you dedicate 30 minutes each day to practice? Could you focus on mastering one new chord each week? Could you record yourself playing and listen back to hear your improvement? Absolutely! The point is, that dedication and consistent effort are like the ultimate powers. They can help you achieve things you never thought possible, whether you're on the basketball court, in the classroom, or anywhere else in life.

But here's the really important part— it's not always going to be easy. There will be days when you don't feel like practicing. Days when you'd rather hang out with friends or binge-watch your favorite show. And that's okay! We all have those days. The key is to push through them. Remember why you started in the first place. Remember your goals. Remember how good it feels to see yourself improve.

So here's your challenge: Take a moment to think about your own practice routines. Whether it's for basketball, schoolwork, or any other skill you're trying to improve. Are you being dedicated? Are you putting in consistent effort? Or are you just going through the motions?

If you're not where you want to be, that's okay! The great thing about dedication and consistent effort is that you can start applying them right now. Today. This very moment. You don't need any special equipment or skills. All you need is the willingness to put in the work. Remember, every great player, every straight-A student, every rock star guitarist—they all started as beginners. The only difference between them and everyone else is that they never stopped practicing, never stopped improving, and never stopped believing in themselves.

So set your goals, make your schedule, and get to work. It won't always be easy, but I promise you, it'll be worth it.

Who knows? Maybe one day, we'll be telling your story to inspire the next generation.

CHAPTER 3:

Teamwork and Leadership

Being a superstar player with all the fancy moves and the killer crossover? That's only half the battle. The real magic happens when you can take that individual talent and use it to elevate your entire team.

You see, basketball isn't just about flashy dunks and three-pointers. It's about coming together, working as one, and pushing each other to be the best versions of ourselves. And when you've got a true leader on your squad—someone who can inspire the troops, call the shots, and bring out the best in everyone—that's when the real winning starts.

In this chapter, we're going to explore two legends who embody the power of teamwork and leadership—Magic Johnson and Phil Jackson. Now, these guys didn't just sit back and let their natural talent carry them to the top. Nope, they put in the work, they built the bonds, and they orchestrated some of the most legendary runs in basketball history. Let's start with the basics— what exactly do we mean by teamwork and leadership in basketball? Well, it's all about working

together, communicating, and putting the team's goals above your own personal glory.

Think about it this way: Basketball is a team sport, plain and simple. You can have the most talented player on the court, but if they're not willing to share the ball, listen to their teammates, and make that extra pass, they're not going to get very far. Teamwork is what transforms a group of individuals into a well-oiled machine. And when it comes to leading that machine, that's where the real magic happens. A true leader in basketball isn't just the one who scores the most points or pulls down the most rebounds. Nope, a real leader is the one who can inspire their teammates, strategize the game plan, and bring out the best in everyone around them.

How many times have you seen a team full of superstars fail, simply because they couldn't get on the same page? Yeah, it happens all the time. But then you look at the teams that dominate year after year, and you realize they've got that special something that goes beyond individual talent.

That's where leaders like Magic Johnson and Phil Jackson come in. These guys didn't just show up and do their own thing. They brought their teams together, got everyone rowing in the same direction, and turned potential into championships. And that, my friends, is yet another great secret of basketball greatness.

So, get ready to be inspired, chaps. Because when you see what these two titans of the game were able to accomplish, you're going to realize that individual skill is good, but teamwork and leadership? That's what takes you from good to great.

Magic Johnson: The Maestro of Teamwork

Now, when you think of basketball legends, Magic Johnson's name has got to be near the top of the list. Now, he's got a story that'll make your jaw drop faster than a sick crossover.

Let's head back to the 1980s! There's this dude on the court who's got everyone's heads spinning. We're talking about Earvin "Magic" Johnson, the maestro of the hardwood, the wizard of assists, the sultan of teamwork! This guy wasn't just playing basketball—he was conducting a full-on hoops symphony!

"Sure, Magic was great, but what made him so special?"

First off, let's talk about Magic's passing game. This guy had eyes in the back of his head, I swear! He could thread the needle through the tiniest gaps, finding teammates who didn't even know they were open yet! It was like he had some kind of basketball ESP or something!

Fun Fact Alert! Did you know Magic once dished out 24 assists in a single game? That's like handing out high-fives to every single player on the court... twice! And get this—he averaged

11.2 assists per game over his entire career. That's higher than most players' scoring averages!

But ol' Magic wasn't just about flashy passes and no-look dimes. Nope! This guy was all about making his teammates better. He was like a basketball Midas—everything he touched turned to gold! With Magic running the show, the Lakers' "Showtime" era was born, and boy, was it a sight to behold! Just picture this for a moment: You've got Kareem Abdul-Jabbar, the sky-hook master. James Worthy, the original Big Game James. Byron Scott, raining threes before it was cool. And there's Magic, orchestrating it all like a hoops maestro. It was like watching basketball poetry in motion!

Here's another mind-blowing fact for ya: During Magic's 13-year career, the Lakers made it to the NBA Finals a whopping 9 times! That's like making the honor roll every single year of high school... and then some!

But Magic wasn't just about winning games. He was about changing the game itself. Before Magic came along, point guards were supposed to be these small, speedy guys who just dribbled the ball up the court. But Magic? He burst onto the scene at 6'9", handling the rock like a pro and seeing over defenders like they were toddlers! In his very first NBA Finals game as a rookie, Magic started at center! Yeah, you heard that right—a point guard playing center! And you know what he did? He dropped 42 points, grabbed 15 rebounds, and dished out 7 assists. Talk about versatility!

Now, let's talk about Magic's leadership skills, 'cause this is where he really shined brighter than a freshly polished trophy.

Magic had this infectious energy that could light up an entire arena. He was like a human Red Bull, bouncing around the court with a million-dollar smile, hyping up his teammates, and making everyone believe they could fly! And you know what? That belief translated into championships. With Magic at the helm, the Lakers snagged five NBA titles in the 1980s. That's like winning the school talent show five years in a row—absolutely bonkers!

But here's the thing that really set Magic apart: he didn't care about being the top dog. This guy was all about the team. He'd pass up an open shot to get a teammate an even better look. He'd dive for loose balls like his life depended on it. He played with a joy and passion that was simply contagious.

Wanna know how much Magic cared about his team?

In 1985, he took less money on his contract so the Lakers could afford to keep key players. That's right—he put the team's success above his own paycheck. Now that's what I call a true leader!

So, what can we learn from Magic's incredible journey?

Well, for starters, it's a slam dunk reminder that being a great baller isn't just about how many points you can score. It's about making everyone around you better too. It's about seeing the big picture and understanding that when the team wins, everybody wins.

Think about it: How many times have you been part of a group project where everyone's just doing their own thing? It's a mess, right? But imagine if you had someone like Magic in your group —someone who could bring everyone together, make sure everyone's strengths were being used, and keep everyone hyped and motivated. That's the kind of leadership that turns good teams into great ones!

And here's the coolest part—you don't need to be a 6'9" basketball prodigy to be like Magic. His lessons apply to everything in life! Whether you're captain of your school's debate team, leader of a group project, or just trying to rally your friends for a pickup game, you can channel your inner Magic.

Greatness isn't just about what you can do—it's about what you can inspire others to do. That's the real magic of teamwork and leadership. So the next time you're feeling like you're just one small player in a big game, think about Magic Johnson. Think about how he took a bunch of talented individuals and turned them into an unstoppable force. Think about how he understood that true greatness comes from lifting others up.

Because when you tap into that Magic-style leadership, there's no limit to what you and your team can achieve. Whether it's on the basketball court, in the classroom, or just in everyday life, the power to bring people together and inspire them to greatness— that's the kind of superpower that can change the world.

You've got that same magic inside of you, too. You just have to tap into it, unleash it, and let it shine. Go out there, be a team player, be a leader, and show the world what you're made of.

Phil Jackson—The Zen Master's Coaching Philosophy

Now, if Magic Johnson was the maestro of teamwork on the court, then Phil Jackson was the sensei of coaching, taking the game to a whole new level with his unorthodox yet highly effective approach.

In the 1990s there's this dude on the sidelines who looks more like a college professor than a basketball coach. But don't let that fool you—Phil Jackson was about to school everyone on how to win championships like it was going out of style!

"Sure, Phil won a bunch of rings, but what made him so special?"

Just hold onto your jerseys, 'cause we're about to break it down faster than a Scottie Pippen fast break!

First off, let's talk about Phil's crazy coaching style. This guy wasn't just drawing Xs and Os on a whiteboard—he was channeling his inner Yoda and bringing some serious Jedi mind tricks to the basketball court! Can you believe he actually had his players meditate before games? That's right, while other teams were pumping iron, Phil's squad was saying "Ommmm" and finding their inner peace!

Fun Fact Alert! Phil once made the entire Bulls team sit in silence for an hour before a big playoff game. Michael Jordan thought he was nuts, but guess what? They won by 20 points! Talk about mind over matter!

But Phil wasn't just about meditation and mindfulness. This guy was like a basketball psychologist, figuring out what made each player tick and then using that knowledge to push all the right buttons. He'd give books to his players—not playbooks, but actual books about philosophy and spirituality. Can you imagine Shaq curled up with a copy of "Zen and the Art of Motorcycle Maintenance"? Now that's a mental image! Speaking of Shaq, let's talk about how Phil managed to wrangle some of the biggest egos in NBA history. We're talking Michael Jordan, Scottie Pippen, Dennis Rodman, Kobe Bryant, Shaquille O'Neal—this guy coached more superstars than a Hollywood agent! And somehow, he got them all to play nice together (well, most of the time).

When Phil took over the Bulls in 1989, Michael Jordan was already a superstar, but the team couldn't get past the Detroit Pistons in the playoffs. Phil came in with his "triangle offense" (more on that in a sec), and suddenly the Bulls were unstoppable! They went from perennial playoff losers to winning six championships in eight years. That's like going from the bottom of your class to valedictorian... times six!

Now, about that triangle offense—this was Phil's secret weapon, his basketball equivalent of a Jedi lightsaber. It was a system that emphasized teamwork, ball movement, and reading the defense. Most coaches would just give the ball to their best player and say, "Go score!" But not Phil. He wanted everyone involved, everyone touching the ball, everyone being a threat.

Fun Fact Time! The triangle offense was so complex that even some of Phil's own players didn't fully understand it. Dennis Rodman once said something along the lines, "I don't know anything about the triangle. I just go out there and rebound." And you know what? It still worked!

And, Phil didn't just use this system with one team. He took it to the Lakers and won five more championships! That's like acing the same test with two completely different study groups!

Now, let's talk about some of Phil's craziest coaching moments, 'cause this guy was anything but conventional:

- **The incense incident:** Phil once lit incense in the locker room before a game to "cleanse the air." The players thought the building was on fire!

- **The Native American rituals:** Phil would sometimes use Native American spiritual practices with his teams. He once had the Bulls participate in a "vision quest" during training camp. Imagine Michael Jordan in war paint—now that's a sight!

- **The nickname game:** Phil was the king of giving weird nicknames to his players. He called Shaquille O'Neal "Big Aristotle" and Kobe Bryant "Little Flying Warrior." Talk about mind games!

- **The silent treatment:** During one particularly frustrating game, Phil didn't say a word during timeouts. He just sat there, staring at his players. And you know what? They figured it out and won the game!

- **The book club:** Phil would assign different books to his players based on their personalities. He once gave Dennis Rodman a book about Native American philosophy. Rodman's response? "I don't read." Classic Rodman!

But it wasn't all smooth sailing in Phil's Zen basketball world. Oh no, he had his fair share of challenges. Like the time Kobe and Shaq were at each other's throats, threatening to tear the Lakers apart. What did Phil do? He wrote a whole book about it! That's right, in the middle of the season, he published "The Last Season," airing all the team's dirty laundry. Most coaches would get fired for that, but Phil? He came back the next year and won another championship!

Or how about the time he left the Lakers, wrote a book criticizing Kobe Bryant, and then came back to coach the team again? Talk about awkward! But somehow, Phil made it work. He and Kobe buried the hatchet (not literally, though with Phil, you never know), and went on to win two more titles together. Here's another mind-blowing Phil fact: He's the only coach in NBA history to win more than 10 championships. Eleven rings, people! That's enough bling to open a jewelry store!

But wait, there's more! Phil wasn't just a basketball guru—he was a pop culture icon. He dated the Lakers' owner's daughter (talk about office romance!), wrote multiple bestselling books, and even had a cameo in the movie "Game of Death" with Bruce Lee. Is there anything this guy couldn't do?

Now, you might be wondering, "How did Phil come up with all these crazy ideas?" Well, it all started back in his playing days. Phil was part of the New York Knicks championship teams in the 70s, playing alongside legends like Walt Frazier and Willis Reed. But he wasn't a superstar—he was a role player, a bench guy who had to outthink his opponents to stay in the league. This experience gave Phil a unique perspective on the game. He saw firsthand how egos could tear a team apart, and how important it was for everyone to buy into a system. So when he became a coach, he was determined to create an environment where every player, from the superstar to the bench warmer, felt valued and important.

And boy, did it work! Phil's teams weren't just successful—they were dynasties. The Bulls of the '90s, the Lakers of the 2000s— these teams didn't just win championships, they dominated entire eras of basketball.

The really crazy part? Phil did it all while looking like he was barely breaking a sweat. While other coaches were screaming and stomping on the sidelines, Phil would just sit there, cool as a cucumber, maybe giving a little smirk when his team hit a big shot. It was like he knew something nobody else did—like he had unlocked the secret to basketball nirvana. And in a way, he had. Phil understood that basketball, like life, was about more than just X's and O's. It was about understanding people, managing emotions, and creating an environment where everyone could thrive. He wasn't just coaching basketball players—he was molding them into better people.

So, the next time you're watching a basketball game and see a coach losing their mind on the sidelines, remember good ol' Phil Jackson. Remember how he turned the NBA upside down with his Zen philosophy and unorthodox methods? Remember how he took a bunch of superstars with giant egos and turned them into cohesive, championship-winning machines?

Let's dive a little deeper into some of the key principles that made Phil Jackson's coaching approach so effective, and how you can apply them to your own life:

- **Embracing Mindfulness and Meditation**

  One of the cornerstones of Jackson's philosophy was the belief in the power of the mind. By incorporating mindfulness and meditation practices into his team's routine, he helped his players stay focused, centered, and in touch with their bodies and their emotions. This, in turn, allowed them to perform at a higher level, both individually and as a team.

○ As you think about applying this to your own life, consider how you can introduce more mindfulness and meditation into your daily routine. Maybe it's taking 10 minutes each morning to sit quietly and focus on your breathing. Or maybe it's trying a guided meditation app to help you manage stress and stay present. The key is to find a practice that works for you and to stick with it, even on the days when it feels challenging.

- **Leveraging Psychological Insights**

In addition to his spiritual leanings, Phil Jackson was also a student of human behavior and psychology. He'd spend hours studying his players, trying to understand their motivations, their triggers, and their unique needs. And then he'd use that knowledge to push them, challenge them, and ultimately bring out the best in them.

○ As you think about your own life and relationships, consider how you can apply some of these psychological insights. Maybe it's learning to better understand the communication styles and personality types of the people you work with. Or maybe it's practicing active listening and empathy to build stronger connections with your teammates or classmates. The more you can learn about human behavior, the better equipped you'll be to navigate the complex social dynamics of any group setting.

- **Fostering a Culture of Collaboration and Trust**

At the heart of Phil Jackson's coaching philosophy was the idea of creating a team culture that emphasized collaboration, communication, and a deep sense of trust.

Instead of relying solely on individual talent, he'd work tirelessly to get his players to buy into a shared vision and to trust in each other's abilities.

○ As you think about your own experiences with teamwork and group dynamics, consider how you can apply these principles. Maybe it's being more proactive about sharing information and seeking input from your teammates. Or maybe it's finding ways to build stronger interpersonal bonds, whether it's through team-building activities or simply making time to socialize and get to know each other better.

The key is to remember that true success, whether it's on the basketball court or in the classroom, is rarely the result of individual heroics. It's about harnessing the collective power of a well-coordinated, cohesive team—and that's exactly what Phil Jackson was able to do, time and time again.

Lesson—The Value of Collaboration and Leading by Example

The truth is that true, lasting achievement, whether it's on the basketball court or in any other area of life, comes from the power of the collective.

"Collaboration? Leading by example? That sounds like a bunch of mushy, feel-good nonsense."

Hear me out, because these are the principles that transformed players like Magic Johnson and Phil Jackson into legends, and they can do the same for you, too.

Let's start with collaboration. What does that really mean in the context of basketball (or any team-based endeavor)? Well, it's all about working together, communicating effectively, and putting the team's goals above your own personal glory. It's about understanding your role, trusting your teammates, and using your unique skills to help the squad shine. And that's exactly what we saw from the greats like Magic and Phil. These guys weren't just talented individuals—they were maestros of teamwork, able to bring the best out of everyone around them.

With Magic, it was all about his ability to make his teammates better. He'd zip those no-look passes, find the open man, and create easy scoring opportunities. But it wasn't just the assists that made him special—it was the way he kept the energy and the tempo up, the way he fostered an environment of trust and camaraderie. And with Phil Jackson, it was his holistic approach to coaching—blending basketball strategy with mindfulness, psychology, and a deep understanding of team dynamics. He didn't just draw up plays; he created a culture of collaboration, where everyone felt empowered to contribute and the whole was greater than the sum of its parts.

These lessons of collaboration and leading by example aren't just limited to the basketball court. Nope, they're applicable to all sorts of group settings, from school projects to youth sports teams to any situation where you need to work with others to achieve a common goal.

So, what are some specific strategies you can use to improve your own teamwork and leadership skills?

- **Communicate Openly and Honestly**

  One of the key foundations of effective collaboration is clear, open communication.

  Make sure you're constantly checking in with your teammates, sharing information, and listening to their ideas and concerns. Don't be afraid to have tough conversations or to provide constructive feedback—just do it in a way that's respectful and focused on the team's best interests. And remember, communication is a two-way street. Be just as willing to share your own thoughts and perspectives as you are to hear out your teammates. The more transparent and honest you can be, the stronger the bonds of trust and understanding will become.

- **Embrace Your Unique Role**

  In any team setting, whether it's basketball or something else, everyone has a different set of skills and strengths to contribute.

  The key is to understand what your unique role is and to embrace it wholeheartedly. Don't worry about being the superstar or the one who gets the glory—focus instead on how you can use your talents to help the team succeed. Maybe you're the facilitator, the one who keeps the group on track and moving forward. Or maybe you're the creative problem-solver, the one who comes up with innovative solutions. Whatever your role may be, own it with pride and make sure you're constantly looking for ways to elevate the collective performance.

- **Lead by Example**

  One of the most powerful ways to demonstrate leadership is through your own actions and behaviors.

  Set the tone with your work ethic, your positive attitude, and your willingness to make sacrifices for the greater good. When your teammates see you putting in the hard work, staying focused, and always putting the team first, it inspires them to do the same. But leading by example isn't just about outworking everyone else. It's also about modeling the kind of collaborative, team-oriented mindset that you want to see from your teammates. Be a communicator, a problem-solver, and a source of encouragement. Show them what it looks like to trust in each other and to believe in the power of the collective.

- **Foster Trust and Camaraderie**

  At the end of the day, true collaboration and effective leadership are built on a foundation of trust and interpersonal connection.

  That's why it's so important to create opportunities for your team to bond, whether it's through team-building exercises or simply hanging out and getting to know each other better. When your teammates feel like they can trust you, and when they know that you've got their backs, it unlocks a whole new level of performance and commitment. They're more willing to take risks, to be vulnerable, and to put the team's needs ahead of their own. And that's the kind of dynamic that can transform a group of individuals into an unstoppable force.

- **Adaptability and Flexibility**

  No plan survives contact with the battlefield, and that's true for teams too.

  The best leaders and teammates are the ones who can roll with the punches, adapt to changing circumstances, and help steer the group through unexpected challenges. Being able to pivot without losing focus on the goal is a next-level skill that sets teams apart.

- **Encourage and Motivate Others**

  Great teams aren't just about getting the job done; they're about lifting each other up along the way.

  When your teammates are struggling or feeling down, step in with encouragement or a pep talk. Being the person who motivates others, especially when the going gets tough, is a crucial way to build morale and keep everyone moving forward.

- **Accountability**

  Accountability isn't just about calling out mistakes; it's about holding yourself and your teammates to a high standard.

  Own your actions, both the wins and the mistakes, and encourage others to do the same. A team where everyone is accountable fosters mutual respect and trust, which leads to more consistent and top-tier performance.

- **Focus on Team Goals Over Personal Glory**

  The ultimate teamwork mindset is realizing that the success of the group is more important than personal accolades.

  It's about trading ego for synergy. Keep your eyes on the shared goals and make sacrifices when needed for the team to win, even if that means stepping back to let others shine.

- **Practice Empathy**

  In any group, you'll have different personalities and perspectives.

  Leaders and great teammates practice empathy by understanding where others are coming from, especially in moments of stress or disagreement. This fosters a sense of inclusivity and helps smooth over conflicts before they escalate.

- **Continuous Improvement**

  Great teams don't settle for "good enough." Always be looking for ways to improve your individual skills and your team's performance. After every project or game, do a debrief. What went well? What could've been better? Then apply those lessons going forward.

- **Celebrate Wins—Big and Small**

  Take time to celebrate victories—whether it's a major success or just a small step in the right direction. Acknowledging achievements boosts morale, keeps motivation high, and reminds the team of the progress being made toward the larger goal.

The good news is that you can start applying these lessons in all sorts of group settings, whether it's a school project, a youth sports team, or even just a group of friends trying to tackle a challenge together.

Maybe it's taking the lead on organizing a team-building activity or volunteering to be the one who keeps the group on track and focused. Or maybe it's simply being the one who's always willing to lend a helping hand or offer encouragement to your teammates. The key is to find small, practical ways to demonstrate the power of collaboration and leading by example. When you start to apply these principles, you'll see the benefits spill over into other areas of your life. Suddenly, that group project at school starts to feel a little less like pulling teeth and a little more like a well-oiled machine. That youth sports team you're on? It's starting to feel less like a collection of individuals and more like a true team.

At the end of the day, the lessons of collaboration and leading by example aren't just about basketball—they're about life. They're about the power of working together, of trusting each other, and of bringing out the best in those around you.

CHAPTER 4:

Handling Pressure

Let's face it, whether you're a superstar like Michael Jordan or just a kid trying to make the school team, pressure is an unavoidable part of basketball (and life in general).

The clock's winding down, the game's on the line, and all eyes are on you. The tension's palpable, your heart's pounding, and the weight of the moment can feel like it's crushing you. But that's where the true greats separate themselves from the rest of the pack. They're the ones who thrive under pressure, who rise to the occasion and deliver when it counts the most.

In this chapter, we're going to explore what it takes to be a clutch performer, to be the one who can keep their cool and make the big play when the stakes are highest. And we're going to do it by looking at two legendary figures—the one and only Michael Jordan, and the 2016 Cleveland Cavaliers team that pulled off one of the most improbable championship comebacks in NBA history.

"Michael Jordan? Handling pressure? Duh, that's a no-brainer."

And you're absolutely right. Jordan's reputation as a clutch performer is the stuff of legend, with a resume that's littered with game-winning shots, playoff heroics, and ice-in-his-veins moments that have cemented his status as one of the greatest athletes of all time. But what's really fascinating is how he was able to do it, game after game, when the stakes were highest. Because let's be real, even for the best of the best, pressure can be a beast. It can make your palms sweat, your mind race, and your legs feel like jelly. But for Jordan, it was almost like he thrived on it.

So, what was his secret?

Well, it all came down to mindset, preparation, and an unrelenting competitive drive. Jordan was a student of the game, constantly studying his opponents, dissecting their weaknesses, and finding ways to exploit them. But more than that, he was a master of his own mental state, able to block out the noise, stay focused, and execute with ice-cold precision when it mattered most. And it wasn't just the game-winning shots that made him special—it was the way he carried himself, the way he embraced the pressure and used it to fuel his performance. Whether it was hitting a last-second jumper to win the NBA Finals or taking over a playoff game with sheer force of will, Jordan had a knack for rising to the occasion and leaving his mark on history.

But as incredible as Jordan's individual exploits were, the 2016 Cleveland Cavaliers showed us that handling pressure isn't just an individual skill—it's a team-wide mentality that can take you to the promised land.

Think about it—the Cavs were down 3-1 to the Golden State Warriors in the NBA Finals, a seemingly insurmountable deficit against one of the most dominant teams in league history. But instead of crumbling under the weight of the moment, the Cavs came together, dug deep, and put together one of the most remarkable comebacks in sports history.

And it wasn't just LeBron James who led the charge—it was the entire team, from Kyrie Irving's clutch shots to Kevin Love's lockdown defense. They trusted in each other, communicated openly, and refused to let the pressure get the better of them. Even when things looked bleak, they kept their cool, stuck to the game plan, and ultimately emerged victorious.

And what can we learn from the Cavs' incredible performance?

Well, for starters, it's a reminder that pressure isn't just an individual battle—it's a team-wide challenge that requires everyone to be on the same page. When you've got that kind of collective focus, determination, and resilience, you can overcome just about anything.

But it's not just about basketball, either. These lessons of handling pressure can be applied to, well, just about any situation where you're faced with high-stakes challenges.

Michael Jordan—The Clutch Performer

Jordan's ability to thrive under pressure wasn't just a product of his sheer talent and athleticism (although let's be real, the guy was a freak of nature). Nope, it was something deeper, something that set him apart from even the greatest players of his era.

It's the final seconds of a championship game, the crowd's going nuts, and everyone's sweating bullets. But there's one dude on the court who's cooler than a polar bear's toenails—yep, you guessed it, it's MJ! This guy didn't just play basketball; he turned pressure into his personal playground!

"Sure, MJ was great, but what made him the ultimate clutch performer?"

Well, you just hang onto your Air Jordans, 'cause we're about to break it down faster than His Airness' first step!

First off, let's talk about Jordan's mentality. This guy didn't just handle pressure—he ate it for breakfast, lunch, and dinner! While most players were shaking in their sneakers, MJ was licking his chops, ready to feast on the competition. It's like the dude had ice water in his veins instead of blood!

Fun Fact Alert! Did you know that in his entire career, Jordan never lost more than two games in a row in the NBA Finals? That's right—when the stakes were highest, MJ was at his best. Talk about clutch!

But MJ's clutch gene wasn't just about natural talent (though let's be real, the guy could fly). Nope, it was all about that mental game. Jordan prepared for pressure situations like a master chess player, always thinking ten moves ahead. He'd visualize every possible scenario, and practice every conceivable shot, and when game time came, he was ready for anything! Jordan once said, "I've missed more than 9,000 shots in my career. I've lost almost 300 games. Twenty-six times, I've been trusted to take the game-winning shot and missed. I've failed over and over and over again in my life. And that is why I succeed." Talk about turning pressure into fuel!

Now, let's break down some of MJ's most epic clutch moments, 'cause this list is longer than his legendary wingspan:

- **"The Shot" (1989 playoffs vs. Cleveland):** With the Bulls down by one and 3 seconds left, MJ hits a hanging jumper over Craig Ehlo to win the series. Ehlo falls to the ground in despair while Jordan leaps into the air, fist-pumping. Ice cold!

- **The "Flu Game" (1997 NBA Finals, Game 5):** Jordan's battling a nasty stomach virus (or was it food poisoning?), looking like he might pass out any second. But he still drops 38 points, including the game-winning three-pointer. Who does that?!

- **The Last Shot (1998 NBA Finals, Game 6):** Down by one, final seconds ticking away. Jordan steals the ball, dribbles down, crosses over Bryon Russell (maybe with a little push-off, but who's counting?), and nails the jumper to clinch his sixth championship. Storybook ending, anyone?

- **63 points against the Celtics (1986 playoffs):** Young MJ goes off against one of the greatest teams ever, in Boston Garden no less. Larry Bird said it was like "God disguised as Michael Jordan." When Larry Legend says that, you know it's legit!

- **The Shrug (1992 NBA Finals, Game 1):** Jordan hits six first-half three-pointers against Portland, then turns to the announcer's table and shrugs as if to say, "I don't know what's happening either!" When you're so hot you surprise yourself, that's next-level clutch!

But Jordan's clutch gene wasn't just about scoring. This guy could lock down the opposing team's best player when it mattered most. Remember the 1991 NBA Finals against Magic Johnson and the Lakers? MJ not only led the Bulls in scoring but also shut down Magic in crucial moments. That's like being the star quarterback and the shutdown cornerback at the same time!

"How did MJ get so clutch?"

Well, it all started way back in his childhood. Little Mike was always competing—against his older brother, against his teammates, and even against himself. He turned everything into a competition, from basketball to ping pong to who could mow the lawn fastest! The interesting thing is that Jordan was actually cut from his high school varsity team as a sophomore. Can you believe it? The greatest player of all time was told he wasn't good enough! But instead of giving up, MJ used that rejection as fuel. He practiced harder than ever, made the team the next year, and well... the rest is history!

This competitive fire followed MJ throughout his career. He wasn't just trying to win games; he was trying to dominate his opponents, to break their will. There are countless stories of Jordan trash-talking players, making bets with teammates during games, and even berating his own teammates in practice to toughen them up! Here's a wild one: During a regular-season game against the Utah Jazz, Jordan bet a Bulls assistant coach $5 that he could block 7-foot-2 center Mark Eaton's shot. Next defensive possession, MJ leaves his man, times his jump perfectly, and swats Eaton's shot into the third row. Then he just turns to the bench and holds out his hand for the five bucks. Who does that in the middle of an NBA game?!

But it wasn't just about the competition for MJ. He had this uncanny ability to focus, to block out everything except the task at hand. When the pressure was on, Jordan entered what he called his "zen mode." It was like the rest of the world faded away, and all that was left was him, the ball, and the basket. And the more pressure there was, the calmer Jordan seemed to get. It's like he had this superpower where he could slow down time. While everyone else was rushing and panicking, Jordan was in complete control. He'd see openings that no one else could see, make passes that seemed impossible, hit shots that defied the laws of physics.

Remember the famous "double-nickel" game? It was 1995, Jordan had just come back from retirement, and in only his fifth game back, he drops 55 points on the Knicks. In Madison Square Garden. With the whole world watching. That's like acing a final exam after skipping class for a year! But perhaps the most incredible thing about Jordan's clutch performances was how consistent they were. This wasn't a guy who had one or two big moments—he delivered time and time again, year after year. Six NBA Finals, six championships, six Finals MVPs. When the lights were brightest, MJ shone the brightest.

So what can we learn from Michael Jordan's incredible ability to perform under pressure?

Well, for starters, it's about preparation. Jordan didn't just rely on his natural talents—he worked harder than anyone else, both physically and mentally. He studied his opponents, visualized success, and put in the hours when no one was watching. It's also about mindset. Jordan didn't fear pressure—he embraced it. He saw those high-stakes moments as opportunities to prove himself, to cement his legacy. And when you approach pressure with that kind of attitude, suddenly it becomes a lot less scary.

But most importantly, it's about belief. Jordan had an unshakeable confidence in himself, a belief that no matter how tough things got, he would find a way to come out on top. And time and time again, he proved himself right.

And that's a lesson that goes way beyond basketball, my friends. Because let's be real, pressure isn't just something you face on the court—it's a constant companion in all areas of life. Whether it's a big exam, a high-stakes job interview, or a personal challenge that's testing your limits, the ability to stay calm, focused, and confident in the face of adversity is an invaluable skill.

So, what can you do to start developing your own Michael Jordan-esque approach to handling pressure?

Here are a few key strategies to consider:

- **Cultivate a Winning Mindset**

  One of the things that set Jordan apart was his unshakable belief in himself and his abilities. He didn't just hope for success—he expected it. And that kind of mental toughness and self-confidence can be cultivated through consistent practice and a commitment to continuous improvement.

○ Start by visualizing yourself succeeding in high-pressure situations. Imagine the sights, the sounds, the physical sensations—and then see yourself rising to the occasion and delivering as if you are truly living it. The more you can reinforce that positive mental image, the more naturally it will start to manifest in your actual performance.

- **Master Your Preparation**

  Just like Jordan, make sure you're putting in the work to get ready for those pressure-packed moments. Study your opponents, analyze their tendencies, and find ways to exploit their weaknesses. Hone your skills, refine your game plan, and trust that your preparation will carry you through.

  ○ And remember, it's not just about the physical preparation —it's about the mental preparation, too. Develop routines and habits that help you get into the right headspace, whether it's meditation, deep breathing, or simply taking a few moments to visualize your success.

- **Channel Your Competitive Fire**

  Let's be real, pressure can be a beast. It can make your palms sweat, your heart race, and your legs feel like jelly. But for the greats like Jordan, pressure wasn't something to be feared— it was a challenge to be embraced.

  ○ Tap into that same competitive fire, that burning desire to be the best. Use the pressure as fuel, as motivation to push yourself to new heights. And remember, pressure isn't just about the big, dramatic moments—it's about the grind, the day-in, day-out commitment to being the best version of yourself.

- **Stay Poised and Focused**

  Even when the stakes are highest, even when the crowd is roaring and the game's on the line, Jordan never seemed to lose his cool. He stayed poised, he stayed focused, and he executed with a level of precision and confidence that was truly awe-inspiring.

  - Learn from his example. When the pressure's on, take a deep breath, block out the noise, and trust in your preparation. Stay present, stay disciplined, and don't let the moment overwhelm you. Because at the end of the day, pressure is just another challenge to be conquered—and with the right mindset and approach, you can do it.

The next time you find yourself facing a high-pressure situation, whether it's on the basketball court or in any other area of your life, remember the legend of Michael Jordan. Remember how he rose to the occasion, time and time again, and cemented his status as one of the greatest competitors of all time. Total goosebumps!

2016 Cleveland Cavaliers—Historic Comeback in the NBA Finals

I've got an epic tale for you—one that's sure to get your adrenaline pumping and your competitive juices flowing. Let's rewind the clock to 2016 and the thrilling showdown between the Cleveland Cavaliers and the Golden State Warriors.

The Cleveland Cavaliers are staring down the barrel of a 3-1 deficit in the NBA Finals against the Golden State Warriors. Now, for those of you who don't know, being down 3-1 in the Finals is like being stuck at the bottom of Mount Everest with nothing but flip-flops and a granola bar. It's not just bad—it's "call your mama and tell her you love her" bad!

But this Cavs team wasn't about to roll over and play dead. Nuh-uh! Led by the one and only LeBron James (aka King James, aka The Chosen One, aka... well, you get the picture), these guys were about to show the world what true grit and determination look like!

Fun fact alert! Before the 2016 Cavs, no team in NBA history had ever come back from a 3-1 deficit in the Finals. That's right

Now, let's break down this epic comeback, game by game, 'cause trust me, every moment is worth savoring:

- **Game 5: The Awakening**

  Down 3-1 and playing on the Warriors' home court, most teams would've been planning their summer vacations. But not the Cavs! LeBron and Kyrie Irving put on a show for the ages, each dropping 41 points. That's like having two Michael Jordans on your team! The Cavs won 112-97, and suddenly, a glimmer of hope appeared.

  Fun fact: This was the first time in NBA Finals history that two teammates each scored 40+ points in the same game. Talk about picking the right time to make history!

- **Game 6: The Return to The Land**

  Back in Cleveland, with their home crowd behind them, the Cavs came out like a house on fire! LeBron was everywhere —scoring, rebounding, blocking shots, and probably selling hot dogs during timeouts. He finished with 41 points (again!), 11 assists, 8 rebounds, 4 steals, and 3 blocks. That's not a stat line; that's a video game cheat code!

The Cavs won 115-101, and suddenly, the impossible didn't seem so impossible anymore.

- **Game 7: The Miracle in Oakland**

This is it, peeps—winner takes all. Back in Oakland, with 19,596 screaming Warriors fans hoping to see their team close it out. But the Cavs had other plans.

This game was tighter than your grandma's Tupperware seal. Back and forth they went, neither team able to pull away. And then, with less than two minutes left and the score tied at 89-89, it happened. Three of the most iconic plays in NBA history, all in rapid succession:

- **"The Block"**: LeBron, moving faster than a cheetah on Red Bull, comes out of nowhere to swat Andre Iguodala's layup attempt into next week. People are still trying to figure out how he got there so fast!

- **"The Shot"**: Kyrie Irving, with ice in his veins and swagger for days, drills a step-back three-pointer right in Steph Curry's face. Splash!

- **"The Stop"**: Kevin Love, not known for his defense, somehow manages to stay in front of Steph Curry for an eternity (okay, it was like 10 seconds, but it felt like forever), forcing him into a missed three-pointer.

When the final buzzer sounded, the scoreboard read: Cavaliers 93, Warriors 89. The impossible had become possible. The Cavs had done it!

Now, let's talk about what made this comeback so special, 'cause it wasn't just about talent (though there was plenty of that). It was about mental toughness, teamwork, and refusing to give up even when things looked bleaker than a Cleveland winter.

First off, there's LeBron James. This guy played like he was on a mission from the basketball gods. Check out these insane stats from the last three games of the series:

- 41 points, 16 rebounds, 7 assists, 3 blocks, 3 steals (Game 5)

- 41 points, 11 assists, 8 rebounds, 4 steals, 3 blocks (Game 6)

- 27 points, 11 rebounds, 11 assists, 3 blocks, 2 steals (Game 7)

That's not just good; that's "they're gonna make a movie about this" good!

But it wasn't just LeBron. Kyrie Irving was clutch when it mattered most, hitting that game-winning three in Game 7. Kevin Love, despite struggling offensively, came up big with his defense in crucial moments. And role players like Tristan Thompson and J.R. Smith stepped up huge, doing all the little things that don't always show up in the box score.

Fun fact time! The Cavs' comeback was so improbable that at one point, their odds of winning the series were 3.3%. That's like trying to thread a needle while riding a unicycle... blindfolded!

Now, let's dive deeper into what made this comeback truly epic:

- **The mental game:** Being down 3-1 is tough enough, but doing it against a Warriors team that had just set the regular-season record with 73 wins? That's like trying to climb Everest during a blizzard! But the Cavs never lost faith. They approached each game with a "why not us?" attitude that was simply contagious.

- **Adjustments on the fly:** Cavs coach Tyronn Lue made some brilliant moves during the series. He went with smaller lineups to match the Warriors' speed, unleashed LeBron as a point forward, and found creative ways to get Kyrie Irving involved. It was like watching a chess master at work!

- **Home court advantage:** The Cavs' home crowd in Games 3 and 6 was so loud, it registered on the Richter scale! Okay, maybe not really, but it sure felt like it. The energy in Quicken Loans Arena was electric, giving the Cavs a much-needed boost.

- **Unsung heroes:** While LeBron and Kyrie got most of the headlines, guys like Tristan Thompson (who averaged 10 rebounds per game in the series) and J.R. Smith (who hit crucial threes in Games 6 and 7) played huge roles. It was a total team effort!

- **The power of belief:** Even when they were down 3-1, the Cavs never stopped believing. LeBron famously said after Game 4, "I feel confident because I'm the best player in the world." That kind of confidence is contagious!

This comeback wasn't just about basketball. It was about a city, a region, that had been starved for a championship for over half a century. Cleveland's last major sports title before this? 1964, when the Browns won the NFL Championship (before it was even called the Super Bowl!).

So when LeBron raised that trophy and yelled, "Cleveland, this is for you!", it wasn't just a victory celebration. It was 52 years of frustration, heartbreak, and "maybe next year" finally being washed away. Grown men were crying in the streets. Kids who weren't even born the last time Cleveland won anything were dancing on cars. It was pure, unadulterated joy. And let's not forget the storyline of LeBron James himself. This wasn't just any player leading his team to a championship. This was a kid from Akron, Ohio, who had promised to bring a title to his hometown. Who had left for Miami, won two championships there, and then returned to Cleveland with one goal in mind. And now, against all odds, he had done it.

The impact of this championship went far beyond the basketball court. It gave an entire region a sense of pride, a belief that anything is possible if you work hard enough and never give up. Kids in Cleveland who watched this series will remember it for the rest of their lives, carrying with them the lesson that no obstacle is too big to overcome.

So what can we learn from the Cavs' historic comeback? Well, for starters:

- Never give up
- Believe in yourself
- Teamwork makes the dream work
- Embrace the pressure
- Make history

The next time you're facing a seemingly impossible challenge, whether it's on the basketball court or in life, remember the 2016

Cleveland Cavaliers. Remember how they stared defeat in the face and said, "Not today!" Remember how they shocked the world and proved that with enough heart, determination, and teamwork, anything is possible.

Because that's what champions do. They don't just play the game —they change it. They rewrite the rules, redefine what's possible, and inspire generations to come.

It's all about performing under pressure and staying focused when the stakes are at their highest. In life, there's going to be plenty of times when the fence is down and the odds are stacked against you. But it's how you respond to those challenges that truly defines your character.

Lesson—Performing Under Pressure and Staying Focused

"Performing under pressure? Staying focused? That's easier said than done, coach!"

And you're absolutely right. But the truth is, these are the qualities that separate the good players from the great ones. It's what allows you to hit the game-winning shot, nail the crucial free throws, or make that clutch defensive stop.

Think about LeBron James and the Cavaliers in that 2016 Finals series. They were facing the ultimate pressure cooker, staring down a 3-1 deficit against a team that had just set the record for the most wins in a single NBA season. But instead of crumbling under the weight of those expectations, they rose to the occasion, drawing strength from their unbreakable bond as a team. And it wasn't just LeBron—the entire Cavaliers roster stepped up, with guys like Kyrie Irving and Kevin Love making crucial contributions when it mattered most. They didn't get rattled by the bright lights or the deafening roar of the crowd. Instead, they stayed focused on the task at hand, executing their game plan with precision and determination.

"Well, I'm no LeBron."

You don't need to be. My young friends, it's all about building the right mental and physical foundations.

- **Build Your Pressure-Resistant Foundation**

    First and foremost, it's about practice, practice, practice. I'm talking about the kind of grueling, monotonous drills that might seem boring at the moment, but they're the secret ingredient that'll make you clutch when the pressure's on. Think about it—when you've got that free throw to win the game, do you think you're going to be nervous if you've already sunk a thousand just like it in the gym? Heck no!

    o **Takeaway for life:** Whether you're prepping for a big test or stepping up for a school presentation, it's all about reps. Practice until it's second nature. That way, when the big day comes, you're running on autopilot.

- **The Power of Visualization**

    But it's not just about the physical skills, is it? No, the real magic happens in your head. That's why it's so crucial to develop mental toughness and the ability to stay focused, even when the world around you is spinning out of control. One strategy I always recommend is visualization:

○ Close your eyes and picture yourself in the pressure-packed moment—the game on the line, the crowd going wild, the ball in your hands.

○ See yourself making the play, and feel the adrenaline coursing through your veins.

○ Fully engage every single sense you have—smell it, hear it, touch it, see it, taste the victory! The more you can immerse yourself in that mental simulation, the more prepared you'll be when the real thing happens.

○ **Takeaway for life:** Picture yourself acing that exam or owning that stage at the school talent show. When you can see yourself succeeding, your brain believes it can happen, and it's game on!

- **Positive Self-Talk Is Your Hype Playlist**

And let's not forget about the power of positive self-talk, either. Yeah, I know it might sound a little cheesy, but trust me, those little mantras and affirmations can make all the difference. When the doubt starts creeping in, shut it down with a resounding "I've got this!" or "I'm gonna crush this!"

○ **Takeaway for life:** Whether it's a basketball game or facing off with a tough assignment, don't let doubt take the mic. Speak success into existence.

- **Staying Focused in the Chaos**

Pressure makes diamonds, but it can also make a mess if you're not grounded. When the heat is on, find your focus. How? By concentrating on what you can control. Forget the noise, forget the crowd, forget the "what-ifs." Focus on the task—whether it's nailing your form on that shot or staying calm under scrutiny.

○ **Takeaway for life:** Life will throw distractions your way—friends texting during study time, noise around you when you need quiet. Learn to tune it out and zero in on what really matters.

- **Perform Like It's Just Another Day**

Ever notice how the best athletes look calm, even when the stakes are sky-high? It's because they've trained their brains to treat those moments like any other. When you walk up to the line, don't think "This is the shot that wins it all!"—think "This is just another shot I've made a thousand times." This trick helps keep the nerves at bay.

○ **Takeaway for life:** Approach every high-pressure situation like it's just another day in the office. It's just another exam, another presentation, another game—nothing new.

- **Dealing With Failure**

Let's get real—sometimes, you miss the shot. Sometimes, you mess up under pressure. But here's the kicker: that's okay. Failure isn't the end; it's the lesson. Use those moments as fuel to come back stronger next time. LeBron didn't win every game, but he sure learned from every loss.

○ **Takeaway for life:** When life doesn't go your way, don't beat yourself up. Analyze what went wrong and how you can improve for the next shot.

- **Finding Flow Amidst Chaos**

  There's this thing called "flow," where everything clicks. You're in the zone, the world fades away, and you're laser-focused on the task at hand. To get into that state, challenge yourself just enough so you're fully engaged but not overwhelmed. That's your sweet spot, and it's where magic happens.

  o **Takeaway for life:** Whether on the court or in a tough project, find your flow. Stay engaged but don't let the stakes overwhelm you. That's when your best work shines through.

Performing under pressure and staying focused isn't just about basketball—it's a skill that'll serve you well in all aspects of life. These lessons can be applied far beyond the court.

Take a page out of the Cavaliers' playbook. Channel that same unwavering determination, that unbreakable focus, and watch as you start to achieve things you never thought possible.

CHAPTER 5:

Learning from Failure

Failure—it's a word that can strike fear into the hearts of even the bravest young athletes. But you know what? Failure is not only inevitable, it's downright essential on the path to greatness.

In this chapter, we're going to check out some of basketball's biggest stars who have turned their darkest moments into their brightest triumphs.

Failure in this sport can take many forms—losing heartbreaking games, missing clutch shots, or even enduring entire disappointing seasons. But the true champions, the real legends, are the ones who have the courage to dust themselves off, learn from their mistakes, and come back stronger than ever. It's not about how many times you face plant, it's about how many times you get back up and carry on.

And that's exactly what we're going to unpack. From individual superstars to tight-knit squads, you're going to see how failure can actually be the secret ingredient to unlocking your full potential.

So, get ready to be inspired, because we're about to meet two shining examples of what it means to learn from failure and let it transform you.

Giannis Antetokounmpo—Rising from Playoff Disappointments

Let's start with the meteoric rise of Giannis Antetokounmpo, the Milwaukee Bucks' superstar forward. Now, Giannis is known for his dominant play, jaw-dropping athleticism, and infectious energy on the court. But it wasn't always smooth sailing for the "Greek Freak."

It's 2013, and a skinny kid from Athens, Greece, steps onto an NBA court for the first time. Giannis Antetokounmpo – yeah, try saying that name five times fast!—looks more like a deer in headlights than the future "Greek Freak." But man, did this kid have potential. Fast forward a few years, and Giannis is starting to make some noise. He's dunking from what seems like half-court, blocking shots into the nosebleed seats, and making defenders look silly. The regular season? He's owning it. But the playoffs? That's where things get a little sticky.

2017 playoffs—Bucks vs. Raptors. Giannis and his crew jump out to a 2-1 series lead. Everyone's thinking, "This is it! The Greek Freak's gonna feast!" But nope. The Raptors flip the script, winning three straight. Giannis and the Bucks? They're watching the rest of the playoffs from their couches.

2018—same story, different year. This time it's the Celtics playing the role of dream-crushers. The Bucks push it to seven games, but in Game 7, they fall flat. Giannis puts up monster numbers, but it's not enough. Cue the critics: "He's just a regular-season player!" "He can't win when it matters!"

Now, here's where a lot of players might crack. The pressure, the disappointment, the doubt—it's enough to make anyone want to curl up in a ball and hide. But Giannis? He's built different. Instead of sulking, he's in the gym. While others are soaking up the sun on some tropical beach, Giannis is working on his jump shot. Free throws? He's shooting hundreds a day. His mindset? "I'm not just gonna be good. I'm gonna be unstoppable."

2019 rolls around, and Giannis is looking like a beast. He's bigger, stronger, and his game's more polished than a freshly waxed floor. The Bucks cruise through the first two rounds of the playoffs. Everyone's thinking, "This is it! The Greek Freak's gonna get his ring!" But hold up—enter the Toronto Raptors, part two. After the Bucks go up 2-0 in the Eastern Conference Finals, the Raptors pull off four straight wins. Giannis and his squad are sent packing... again.

Now, this is where our story could've turned into a tragedy. Three straight years of playoff disappointments? That's enough to break most players. But Giannis? He's not like most players. Instead of hanging his head, he gets back to work. He's in the weight room, on the court, studying film. He's not just working on his game; he's working on his mind. Every missed shot, every lost game, every critic's words—he's using it all as fuel.

2020—another year, another playoff exit. This time it's the Miami Heat playing spoiler. The whispers turn into shouts: "Giannis can't win the big one!" "The Bucks should trade him while they can!"

But here's the thing about Giannis—he doesn't care what anyone else thinks. He knows who he is, what he's capable of, and most importantly, how hard he's willing to work to get there.

And then comes 2021. The year everything changes.

The Bucks storm through the regular season, but everyone's thinking, "Yeah, we've seen this before." First round of the playoffs? They sweep the Miami Heat. Sweet revenge! Eastern Conference Semis? They take down the Brooklyn Nets in a seven-game thriller. Eastern Conference Finals? They send the Atlanta Hawks packing. Suddenly, Giannis and the Bucks find themselves in the NBA Finals. And who's waiting for them? The Phoenix Suns, led by the crafty Chris Paul and the sharpshooting Devin Booker.

Game 1—Suns win. Game 2—Suns win again. Everyone's ready to write off Giannis and the Bucks. "Same old story," they say. But they don't know about all those hours in the gym, all those free throws, all that mental preparation.

Game 3—Bucks win. Game 4—Bucks win again. Series tied!

Game 5—This is where Giannis cements his legacy. With the series hanging in the balance, he pulls off one of the most incredible blocks in NBA Finals history, swatting away what looked like a sure alley-oop. The Bucks win, and suddenly they're one game away from the title.

Game 6—This is it. All those years of disappointment, all those critics, all those doubts—it all comes down to this. And what does Giannis do? He doesn't just show up; he puts on a performance for the ages. 50 points, 14 rebounds, 5 blocks. Oh, and he hits 17 of 19 free throws—remember when everyone said he couldn't shoot?

The final buzzer sounds and it's official: Giannis Antetokounmpo and the Milwaukee Bucks are NBA champions!

But this story isn't just about winning a championship. It's about perseverance. It's about using failure as a stepping stone, not a stumbling block. It's about believing in yourself when no one else does. See, Giannis could've let those playoff losses define him. He could've believed the critics who said he'd never win the big one. But instead, he used every setback as motivation. Every missed shot, every lost game, every harsh word—it all became fuel for his fire.

And that's the real lesson here. Success isn't about never failing; it's about how you respond to failure. Giannis didn't just get better physically; he got tougher mentally. He learned to embrace the pressure, to thrive when the stakes were highest.

So the next time you miss a game-winning shot, or your team loses a big game, remember Giannis. Remember how he turned years of playoff disappointments into the ultimate triumph? Remember that every great player, every true champion, has faced failure on their way to the top. The road to greatness isn't a straight line. It's full of twists and turns, ups and downs. But if you stay committed, if you keep pushing, if you use every setback as motivation to work harder—well, who knows? Maybe one day we'll be telling your story, just like we're telling Giannis's today.

Embrace the setbacks, learn from them, and use them to fuel your relentless pursuit of greatness. Because the road to the top is rarely smooth, but the view from up there is always worth the climb.

San Antonio Spurs—Bouncing Back After 2013 Finals Loss

Wanna hear one of the most epic comeback stories in NBA history? It's a tale of heartbreak, grit, and sweet, sweet redemption. I give you the San Antonio Spurs!

Now, if you don't know the Spurs, you might as well be living under a rock. These guys are like the Beatles of basketball— timeless, legendary, and always in perfect harmony. And the conductor of this basketball orchestra? None other than the grumpy genius himself, Coach Gregg Popovich. Pop, as they call him, is like the wise old wizard of the NBA, except instead of magic spells, he's got plays that'll make your head spin.

It's 2013, and the Spurs are on fire. They've clawed their way to the NBA Finals, facing off against the Miami Heat. And not just any Heat team—we're talking about the LeBron James, Dwyane Wade, Chris Bosh superteam. You know, the guys who made the rest of the league look like a high school JV squad. The series is epic. Back and forth, punch for punch. The Spurs manage to grab a 3-2 lead. They're one win away from their fifth championship. One. Win. Away. Game 6 rolls around, and the Spurs are up by 5 with 28 seconds left. The champagne's on ice, the confetti's ready to fall, and the Larry O'Brien trophy is getting all shined up.

But then... disaster strikes.

In a sequence that still gives Spurs fans nightmares, the Heat's Ray Allen—you know, the guy who never misses—hits a corner three that would make a video game blush. Tie game. Overtime. Spurs lose. Ouch. That's the kind of loss that could break a team. Heck, it could break a whole city. You can almost hear the collective groan from San Antonio to the moon.

Now here's where it gets really good, champs. Because the Spurs? They're built different.

Instead of throwing in the towel or pointing fingers, they did something crazy. They got better. Yeah, you heard me right. They took that loss, that heartbreak, that soul-crushing defeat, and turned it into rocket fuel. Coach Pop, in his infinite wisdom, didn't let the team dwell on the past. Nope. He got them right back to work. While the rest of the world was writing their obituary, the Spurs were in the lab, cooking up something special.

Tim Duncan, the Big Fundamental himself, was in the gym before sunrise, working on his bank shot for the millionth time. Tony Parker was running wind sprints until he could barely stand. Manu Ginobili was probably inventing new ways to pass the ball that defy the laws of physics. But it wasn't just about individual improvement. The Spurs doubled down on what made them special—their teamwork. They passed the ball so much in practice, you'd think it was a hot potato. They ran their plays until they could do them in their sleep. Heck, they probably did do them in their sleep!

And the young guys? Kawhi Leonard and Danny Green? They soaked it all up like sponges. They weren't just learning plays; they were learning how to be champions.

The 2013-2014 season rolls around, and the Spurs are on a mission. They're not just playing basketball; they're playing chess while everyone else is playing checkers. Their offense is like a beautiful dance, with the ball zipping around so fast you'd think it was alive. They storm through the regular season, then the playoffs. Western Conference? More like the Spurs' playground. And before you know it, they're back in the Finals. And guess who's waiting for them? Yep, the Miami Heat. Talk about déjà vu!

But this time? This time it's different. The Spurs aren't just playing basketball; they're exorcising demons. They're turning every possession into a work of art. It's like watching five guys with one brain, moving in perfect sync.

Game 1—Spurs win. But the AC breaks down, and the arena turns into a sauna. LeBron cramps up, and suddenly everyone's talking about air conditioning instead of basketball. But the Spurs? They just keep their cool (pun absolutely intended).

Game 2—Heat strike back. LeBron goes off, and for a moment, everyone's thinking, "Oh no, not again." But the Spurs? They don't panic. They regroup.

Games 3, 4, and 5—This is where the Spurs show the world what they're made of. They don't just win; they dominate. They're passing the ball so well, you'd think they have eyes in the back of their heads. Kawhi Leonard turns into a superstar before our very eyes, locking down LeBron and scoring at will.

And when that final buzzer sounds in Game 5? It's not just a win. It's redemption. It's vindication. It's the sweetest victory you could imagine.

You should've seen the celebration. Tim Duncan, Mr. Stoic himself, actually cracked a smile! Manu Ginobili's bald spot was shining brighter than the Larry O'Brien trophy. Tony Parker was probably already thinking about how to win the next one. In the midst of all that joy, all that celebration, you know what Coach Pop said? He said, "We're just playing basketball." That's it. No grand speeches, no "I told you so's." Just, "We're playing basketball."

And that, my friends, is what makes the Spurs special. They didn't let that 2013 loss define them. They didn't make excuses or point fingers. They just got back to work. They trusted their system, trusted each other, and turned heartbreak into triumph.

So what's the lesson here, young ballers?

It's simple, really. Failure isn't the end of the road; it's just a detour. The Spurs could've let that 2013 loss crush them. They could've broken up the team, fired the coach, and started over. But instead, they used it as motivation. They got better. They got stronger. They got smarter. And that's what champions do. They don't let setbacks set them back. They use them as stepping stones. Every missed shot, every lost game, every heartbreaking defeat—it's all just fuel for the fire.

So the next time you're feeling down, the next time you face a tough loss, remember the Spurs. Remember how they turned the agony of defeat into the thrill of victory. Remember that it's not about never falling; it's about how you get back up.

Because that's what basketball is all about. It's about perseverance. It's about teamwork. It's about believing in yourself and your teammates, even when the whole world is doubting you. The Spurs didn't just win a championship in 2014. They wrote a blueprint for success, for resilience, for never giving up. And who knows? Maybe one day, you'll be the one holding that trophy, thinking back to all the obstacles you overcame to get there.

So get out there and play, but most importantly, never, ever give up. You can't beat someone who never quits.

Lesson—Growth Mindset and Using Setbacks as Motivation

Now, as we've seen from the stories of Giannis Antetokounmpo and the San Antonio Spurs, failure is an inevitable part of the journey to greatness. But the truly remarkable thing is how these athletes and teams responded to their setbacks—they didn't shy away from the challenge, they embraced it and they faced it head-on.

This mindset, this ability to view failures as opportunities for growth and improvement, is what we call the "growth mindset." It's a powerful way of thinking that sets apart the superstars from the also-rans, the champions from the also-rans. You see, the growth mindset is all about that relentless pursuit of betterment, that unshakable belief that no matter how tough the challenge, you can always come back stronger. It's the opposite of the "fixed mindset," where people see their abilities as static and unchangeable, dooming them to repeat the same mistakes over and over again.

A growth mindset is the belief that your abilities, skills, and potential are not set in stone, but can be developed and improved through hard work, dedication, and a willingness to learn from your mistakes. This stands in contrast to a fixed mindset, where people view their talents as unchangeable.

Giannis Antetokounmpo and the San Antonio Spurs exemplified the growth mindset in their respective journeys. When faced with setbacks and failures, they didn't get discouraged or make excuses. Instead, they used those challenges as motivation to push themselves to new levels of excellence. Giannis, for instance, didn't let early playoff disappointments crush his confidence. He doubled down on his training, fine-tuning his skills and physical conditioning, determined to come back better than ever. This mindset ultimately led him to an NBA championship.

Similarly, the Spurs didn't dwell on their heartbreaking loss in the 2013 Finals. They regrouped, refocused, and came back the following season even more unified and determined. Their culture of continuous improvement and resilience allowed them to avenge that defeat and capture the title.

So, what can you take away from these inspiring stories?

It all starts with how you approach failure and adversity. Do you see them as insurmountable obstacles, or as opportunities to grow and improve? The choice is yours, and it can make all the difference in the world.

- **The Power of Self-Reflection**

  When life or a game throws a curveball and you stumble, it's tempting to just brush it off or get frustrated. But here's the winning strategy: stop, take a breath, and reflect. Ask yourself: What went wrong? What can I learn from this? Self-reflection is like having a personal coach in your head, giving you insight and direction. The real magic happens when you analyze your mistakes, learn the lesson, and turn that knowledge into action.

  - **Takeaway for life:** Got a low grade on a test or had a bad game? Instead of beating yourself up, break it down. What can you do better next time? The more you reflect, the sharper your growth mindset gets.

- **Embrace a Lifelong Love for Learning**

  So, you think you've "made it"? Think again. One of the biggest mistakes people make is getting comfortable with where they're at. The best athletes, scholars, and performers know they can always get better. Always. So, what's your game plan? Make continuous learning a part of your routine —whether it's practicing a skill until it's flawless, seeking feedback from coaches or mentors, or studying the greats (your idols), never be satisfied with where you are.

  - **Takeaway for life:** You might be the best on your team right now, but there's always room to grow. Keep leveling up, and before you know it, you'll be breaking your own records. Seek out challenges that force you to grow. Ask questions, study the game, and learn from anyone willing to teach you.

- **Get Comfortable Being Uncomfortable**

  Here's the reality—real growth happens outside your comfort zone. Yeah, the cozy, safe zone feels nice, but it doesn't push you. The magic happens when you tackle the tough stuff head-on. Whether it's taking the big shot in a game, speaking in front of a crowd, or trying a new skill, the more you embrace the tough tasks, the stronger and more adaptable you become.

  o **Takeaway for life:** Don't shy away from what scares you. Whether it's going out for a leadership role, taking a challenging class, or trying something new in a game, that's where growth lives. The more you face your fears, the more resilient you'll be in the long run.

- **Reframe Failure as a Stepping Stone**

  Failure isn't the end of the road, it's just a speed bump. You can't avoid setbacks forever, but you can control how you react to them. Instead of seeing failure as a dead end, think of it as a detour that's redirecting you toward something better. Every stumble is a chance to grow, and every mistake is just another way to learn how not to do something.

  o **Takeaway for life:** Messed up a big play or bombed a quiz? Reframe that moment as a learning opportunity. It's not about perfection—it's about progress. Every failure gets you one step closer to success.

- **Persistence Beats Perfection**

  Perfection? That's a myth. The real champions know that persistence—showing up again and again—is what really counts. It's not about nailing everything on your first try; it's about being relentless, picking yourself up after every fall, and coming back stronger. That persistence is what will push you past adversity and help you crush your goals, even when it feels like the odds are stacked against you.

  o **Takeaway for life:** Whether you're practicing for a sport, studying for exams, or trying to master a new skill, don't chase perfection—chase persistence. Keep showing up, keep trying, and eventually, you'll outlast the challenges that come your way.

- **Surround Yourself with Support**

  Facing adversity alone can feel overwhelming, but you don't have to go it alone. Surround yourself with people who lift you up—teammates, friends, family, or mentors. These are the people who will encourage you when the going gets tough, help you stay grounded, and give you the confidence to keep pushing forward. Your support system is your secret weapon for staying strong in the face of adversity.

  o **Takeaway for life:** If you're struggling, lean on your support system. They've got your back, whether it's friends cheering you on, teachers helping you understand, or mentors guiding you through challenges. You don't have to do it all alone.

At the heart of everything, the real key is having a growth mindset. That means knowing you can get better and that no failure is final. The growth mindset allows you to see every challenge, and every setback, as a stepping stone toward becoming the best version of yourself. With this mindset, you don't fear failure—you welcome it as part of the journey.

So, embrace a growth mindset, use setbacks as fuel for improvement, and never, ever give up on your dreams.

CHAPTER 6:

Breaking Barriers

In the world of basketball, the road to greatness is often paved with those who dare to challenge the status quo, to break down the barriers that others have deemed unbreakable.

It's about individuals who refuse to be defined by preconceived notions, cultural stereotypes, or the limitations that society tries to place upon them.

This chapter is all about those trailblazers, the game-changers who have carved out new paths and paved the way for others to follow. Because make no mistake, the journey to the top is never easy when you're up against deeply entrenched beliefs and biases. But it's those who possess the courage, the determination, and the unshakable conviction to challenge the norms that ultimately leave an indelible mark on the sport, and on the world.

Whether it's physical barriers, cultural divides, or gender-based prejudices, the individuals we're about to explore have demonstrated that with the right mindset and unwavering spirit, no obstacle is too great to overcome. Their stories will inspire you to question the limitations that others have placed upon you, to dream bigger, and to blaze your own trail to greatness.

We're going to focus on two remarkable individuals who have exemplified the power of breaking barriers: Jeremy Lin and Becky Hammon. Lin's journey represents the challenge of overcoming cultural and racial stereotypes as a player, while Hammon's story showcases the fight to break gender barriers in the coaching ranks. We'll see how shattering the status quo in basketball can have a profound impact on societal perceptions and pave the way for others to follow in their footsteps.

It's a testament to the transformative power of those who dare to be different and challenge the limits that others have set for them.

Jeremy Lin—Challenging Stereotypes during "Linsanity"

Let's start with the meteoric rise of Jeremy Lin, a player whose journey captivated the basketball world and inspired a generation of Asian-American youth. This story is part underdog triumph and 100% pure basketball magic—it's the phenomenon known as "Linsanity"!

It's 2012, and the New York Knicks are struggling. They're about as exciting as watching paint dry, and their playoff hopes are fading faster than a cheap jersey in the wash. Enter Jeremy Lin, a guy who's been bouncing around the league like a loose ball, just trying to find his place. Now, Jeremy's not your typical NBA player. He's Asian-American, he's got a degree from Harvard (yeah, that Harvard), and he's been told more times than he can count that he's just not cut out for the big leagues. Too slow, they said. Not athletic enough, they muttered. Doesn't look the part, they whispered.

But here's the thing about Jeremy Lin—he's got more heart than a Valentine's Day card factory. He's been working his tail off, staying ready, just waiting for his chance. And boy, did that chance come in a big way!

The Knicks are hit with a wave of injuries. They're so short-handed, that they're practically holding tryouts in Times Square. Coach Mike D'Antoni, probably thinking, "What the heck, can't get any worse," decides to give Lin some serious playing time.

And what does Jeremy do? He explodes like a basketball supernova!

February 4, 2012—Lin drops 25 points against the Nets. The crowd goes wild. The announcers are scrambling to figure out who this guy is. It's like watching a real-life Rocky movie, only instead of boxing gloves, Lin's got a basketball. But wait, it gets better. Next game? 28 points and 8 assists against the Jazz. The game after that? 23 points and 10 assists against the Wizards. Lin's not just playing well; he's dominating!

And then comes the moment that turns "Linsanity" into a full-blown cultural phenomenon. February 10, 2012—Knicks vs. Lakers. Kobe Bryant and the mighty Lakers come to town, probably thinking they're gonna squash this Cinderella story.

Spoiler alert: They don't.

Lin goes off for 38 points, outdueling Kobe Bryant—yeah, that Kobe Bryant—and leading the Knicks to victory. Madison Square Garden is rocking like it's 1973 all over again. The crowd's going nuts, Lin's teammates are losing their minds, and somewhere in LA, Jack Nicholson is probably spitting out his popcorn in disbelief. Overnight, Jeremy Lin becomes the hottest thing in New York since pizza. His jersey is flying off the shelves faster than they can make them. Every Asian-American kid from coast to coast is suddenly dreaming of playing in the NBA. Lin's face is on every magazine cover, every sports show, heck, probably on a few billboards in Times Square.

And it even gets more real, champs. "Linsanity" wasn't just about basketball. It was about breaking barriers. Smashing stereotypes. Proving that greatness can come from the most unexpected places. Lin wasn't just battling opponents on the court. He was battling perceptions. The idea that Asian Americans couldn't excel in basketball. The notion that if you didn't fit a certain mold, you couldn't make it in the NBA. Every crossover, every three-pointer, every clutch play was a statement. A big, bold, capital letter statement that said, "I BELONG HERE."

And let me tell you, young champions, that message resonated. It echoed through playgrounds in Chinatown, through high school gyms in suburban America, through the dreams of kids who'd been told they were too this or not enough that. Lin's success opened doors. It changed conversations. Suddenly, scouts weren't just looking at the usual suspects. Coaches were rethinking their assumptions. And a whole generation of kids was daring to dream bigger than they ever had before.

But Lin didn't just rest on his laurels. He kept working. Kept improving. Even as "Linsanity" was at its peak, he was in the gym, refining his game, determined to prove that this wasn't just a flash in the pan.

And you know what?

He did prove it. Over the years, Lin carved out a solid NBA career. He may not have maintained that stratospheric level of play from those magical few weeks, but he showed that he belonged. He became a role model, a trailblazer, a living, breathing example of what's possible when you refuse to let others define your limits.

"But what about the pressure? The expectations? The weight of representing an entire community?"

And you're right—that stuff was real. Lin felt it. He talked about it. The pressure to perform, to live up to the hype, to be a perfect role model—it was intense.

But here's where Lin's story gets even more inspiring. He didn't crumble under that pressure. He embraced it. He used it as fuel. Sure, there were ups and downs. Games where he struggled. Seasons where things didn't go as planned. But through it all, Lin kept pushing, kept evolving, kept showing up. And in doing so, he taught us all a valuable lesson. Success isn't about being perfect. It's not about living up to everyone else's expectations. It's about being true to yourself, working your hardest, and making the most of every opportunity that comes your way.

Lin's journey reminds us that stereotypes are meant to be broken. That the only limits that truly matter are the ones we place on ourselves. That with enough hard work, determination, and a little bit of luck, anything is possible.

So the next time someone tells you that you can't do something, remember Jeremy Lin. Remember how he went from the end of the bench to the top of the world. Remember how he turned doubters into believers, and skeptics into fans. And most importantly, remember that your story is still being written. Maybe you're not the tallest, or the fastest, or the most naturally gifted. Maybe you don't fit the traditional mold of what an athlete "should" look like. But guess what? Neither did Jeremy Lin. And look what he did.

Get out there and chase your dreams, no matter how crazy they might seem. Work harder than everyone else. Stay ready for your moment. And when that moment comes, seize it with both hands and don't let go.

Break down barriers, and show the world what's possible when you dare to be different. In basketball and in life, it's not about how you start. It's about how you finish. And if Jeremy Lin taught us anything, it's that the most amazing finishes often come from the most unexpected beginnings.

The world is waiting to see what you can do!

Dare to be different, challenge the norms, and never let anyone tell you that you can't achieve your dreams.

Becky Hammon—First Full-Time Female Assistant Coach in the NBA

While Jeremy Lin's journey challenged cultural stereotypes on the court, the story of Becky Hammon is a testament to the power of breaking down gender barriers in the traditionally male-dominated world of professional basketball coaching.

Now, it's 2014, and the NBA is as male-dominated as a monster truck rally. The idea of a woman coaching in the league? About as likely as finding a vegetarian at a Texas BBQ. But then along comes Becky Hammon, ready to flip the script and rewrite the playbook on what an NBA coach looks like.

Becky's no rookie to the hardwood, mind you. She's been balling since she could walk, tearing it up in the WNBA like a boss. We're talking six-time All-Star, championship winner with the San Antonio Stars. This woman's got more basketball knowledge in her pinky than most folks have in their whole body. But Becky's not content with just dominating on the court. She's got her sights set on the sidelines. And not just any sidelines, mind you. She's aiming for the big leagues, the NBA itself.

Now, let me paint you a picture of what Becky's up against. Imagine trying to break into a boys' club that's been boys-only since, well, forever. We're talking about a league where the closest thing to a female presence on the bench was the occasional courtside reporter. It's like trying to convince a group of lifelong steak lovers to go vegan—not exactly a walk in the park.

But Becky? She's not here for walks in the park. She's here to run marathons and climb mountains.

Enter the San Antonio Spurs and their legendary coach, Gregg Popovich. Now, Pop's not your average coach. He's like the Yoda of basketball, if Yoda traded his robe for a suit and his lightsaber for a clipboard. And Pop sees something in Becky that others might have missed. He doesn't see a woman trying to coach men's basketball. He sees a basketball mind, pure and simple. So, in 2014, Pop does something that shakes the NBA to its core. He hires Becky Hammon as a full-time assistant coach. Boom! Just like that, history is made. The first full-time female assistant coach in any of the four major North American professional sports leagues. It's like the basketball equivalent of landing on the moon.

Now, you'd think everyone would be jumping for joy, right? Wrong. The skeptics come out of the woodwork faster than fans rushing for free t-shirts.

"Can a woman really coach men?" they ask. "Will the players listen to her?" they wonder.

It's like they forgot that basketball doesn't care what chromosomes you have – it only cares if you know the game. But here's where Becky shows she's got more grit than a sandpaper factory. She doesn't let the doubters get her down. Nope, she puts her head down and gets to work. She's in the film room before the rooster's crow, breaking down game tape like it's her job (which, you know, it is). She's on the court, running drills, giving pointers, proving with every whistle-blow that she belongs. And you know what? The players start to notice. They see a coach who knows her stuff, who can break down their game and build it back up better than before. They see someone who's there to make them better, not to make a statement. Before long, Becky's not "the female coach" anymore. She's just Coach Hammon, as much a part of the Spurs as the black and silver jerseys.

Becky's impact goes way beyond the Spurs' practice court. She becomes a beacon of hope for every girl who's ever been told she can't do something because of her gender. Suddenly, young women everywhere are looking at the NBA sidelines and thinking, "Hey, I could do that too!" And it's not just in basketball. Becky's success starts a ripple effect across all sports. Other teams start to realize that maybe, just maybe, they've been missing out on a whole lot of talent by sticking to the old boys' club model. Before you know it, we're seeing women coaching in the NFL, MLB, you name it.

But let's be real—it wasn't all smooth sailing. Becky had to work twice as hard to get half the respect. Every decision she made was under a microscope. If she succeeded, it was because she was good. If she failed, it was because she was a woman. Talk about a double standard!

You know what? Becky took it all in stride. She didn't just meet expectations—she slam-dunked over them. In 2015, she became the first woman to coach an NBA Summer League team. And guess what? Her team won the whole dang tournament! It's like she took all those doubts and turned them into confetti. Fast forward a few years, and Becky's name starts popping up for head coaching jobs. She's interviewing for positions, breaking down even more barriers. And even though she hasn't landed that top job yet (as of my last update), the fact that she's in the conversation is a win in itself.

But here's the real kicker, folks. Becky Hammon's story isn't just about basketball. It's about challenging the status quo. It's about looking at the way things have always been done and asking, "Why not differently?" It's about proving that talent, knowledge, and leadership don't have a gender.

So what's the lesson here? It's simple: Don't let anyone tell you what you can or can't do based on who you are. Whether you're a girl who wants to coach in the NBA, a boy who wants to be a ballet dancer, or anyone who's ever been told "That's not for you"—take a page out of Becky's playbook.

Work hard. Know your stuff. Be so good they can't ignore you. And when you get your shot, don't just take it—slam dunk it.

Every time you step on that court, every time you pick up that clipboard, you're not just playing a game or coaching a team. You're making a statement. You're saying, "I belong here, and I'm going to prove it." Becky Hammon didn't just open a door— she kicked it down and held it open for others to follow.

Dream big, work hard, and never, ever let someone else's limitations become your own. In life, it's not about who you are slam dunkit's about what you can do. And if Becky Hammon taught us anything, it's that you can do anything you set your mind to.

Becky Hammon's accomplishments cannot be overstated. She didn't just break a barrier; she demolished it, leaving an indelible mark on the sport of basketball and inspiring a new generation of young people to dream big, regardless of their background or gender.

Lesson—Courage to be Different and Make a Positive Impact

The true measure of greatness is not just what you achieve, but how you go about it. These individuals didn't just excel in their respective fields; they did so in the face of overwhelming odds, breaking down barriers and challenging the status quo in the process.

At the heart of their stories lies a quality that is both admirable and essential: courage. The courage to be different, to defy the limitations that others have placed upon you, and to forge your own path to success. It's a quality that transcends the boundaries of sports, one that can be applied to every aspect of our lives. But courage alone is not enough. True greatness, the kind that leaves a lasting impact, is about using that courage to make a positive difference in the world around you. It's about using your platform, your talents, and your voice to inspire others, to challenge ingrained biases, and to pave the way for a more inclusive and equitable future.

Courage is the ability to face challenges, take risks, and stand up for what you believe in, even in the face of adversity or criticism. It's about having the conviction to be true to yourself and refuse to be defined by the limitations that others have set for you.

Jeremy Lin and Becky Hammon demonstrated immense courage throughout their respective journeys. Lin refused to be pigeonholed by racial stereotypes, while Hammon shattered gender barriers to become the first full-time female assistant coach in the NBA. But their stories are more than just about personal triumph. Lin and Hammon used their platforms to make a positive impact, inspiring others who faced similar challenges and paving the way for greater representation and opportunity in the world of basketball.

So, how can you cultivate this powerful combination of courage and positive impact in your own life?

- **Your uniqueness is your superpower:** You don't need to fit the mold; in fact, it's better if you don't. The world doesn't need more of the same—it needs you, with all your quirks, talents, and perspectives. It's easy to feel like you have to be a certain way or look a certain way to succeed, but the truth is, the most courageous people are those who lean into their differences and turn them into strengths.

  Whether it's your size, your background, or even your personality, embrace it all. That's what sets you apart. Stand out, don't blend in—and let your individuality shine as you pursue your passions.

- **Courage isn't just about believing in yourself—it's also about putting in the work to back it up:** It's easy to let doubt creep in when you hear "You're not enough," but courage comes from putting in the sweat equity. Whether you're an athlete, artist, or student, practice, train, and study harder than anyone else. Don't just show up—show up prepared, knowing you've worked for every bit of your success.

When someone tells you, "You can't," your preparation will prove them wrong. The more you refine your skills, the more your confidence grows, and soon enough, the naysayers won't even matter.

- **Limits only exist if you let them:** Whether they come from external voices or the little voice inside your head that says "Maybe they're right," courage is about refusing to be boxed in. It's about having the tenacity to push past those limitations, to see how far you can go, and to never stop. Some of the greatest achievements in history came from people who refused to be limited by society's expectations— so why should you be any different?

Every time you face a limitation, remind yourself: this is not the end, it's just another hurdle. Every hurdle you jump only makes you stronger.

- **Here's the most powerful part of courage: once you've achieved something great, you don't stop there:** Courage doesn't just live within you—it spreads. When you've broken through a barrier, look around and see who else needs a hand. Whether it's mentoring a younger player, volunteering in your community, or standing up for inclusivity in your school or sport, true courage means using your voice, your success, and your platform to create a path for others who might be struggling like you once were.

It's not just about what you achieve—it's about the impact you leave on those around you. Be the person who lifts others up as you climb, who offers a hand to those facing the same doubts you once conquered.

- **Success isn't just personal; it's about transforming the world around you:** When you've fought your way to the top, don't let the world stay the same. Courage is about using your influence to push for greater inclusivity, diversity, and fairness in whatever field you're passionate about. Advocate for policies that ensure more voices are heard and more opportunities are given to those who've been overlooked or underestimated.

  Once you've proven yourself, don't just rest on your success —use it. Use your position, your voice, and your story to make sure others get the same shot at greatness, no matter where they come from or what obstacles they face.

- **Courage isn't a one-time thing—it's a daily practice:** Every time you face a new challenge, a new doubt, or a new obstacle, you'll need to summon that courage again. The more you practice pushing back against limitations, the more natural it becomes. Courage is a muscle—use it, and it grows stronger.

  Courage isn't a one-and-done thing. Every new challenge will require it, and each time you face those challenges head-on, you're building a legacy of strength and resilience.

By checking all these boxes, you'll not only realize your own dreams, but you'll also inspire a new generation of trailblazers to follow in your footsteps.

So, my young ballers, take a deep breath, summon your courage, and get ready to make your mark. The future is yours for the taking—go out there and seize it.

Surprise!

Think you've learned all the pro secrets? Not so fast! There's a hidden MVP waiting just for you! Grab your smartphone and scan this QR code—you'll unlock a special collection of pro tips that even some pros don't know about! It's like finding a rare rookie card in your collection, but even better. What's waiting on the other side? Let's just say it's exciting!

CONCLUSION

Alright, we've covered a lot of ground in these past few chapters —from overcoming adversity to breaking down barriers. But as we reach the end, I want you to take a step back and really soak in all that you've learned.

Every story we've explored isn't just about basketball - they're about life. These are the lessons that can propel you to greatness, no matter what challenges you face, both on and off the court.

Let's do a quick recap, shall we? First up, we've got resilience in the face of adversity, embodied by the likes of Derrick Rose and LeBron James. These superstars knew that setbacks were inevitable, but they refused to let them define them. They dusted themselves off, learned from their mistakes, and came back stronger than ever. And then there's the power of practice, exemplified by Kobe Bryant and Stephen Curry. These guys didn't just show up and dominate—they put in the long, grueling hours, honing their skills and pushing the boundaries of what was possible. Dedication and consistent effort, my friends, that's the secret sauce.

Now, let's talk about teamwork and leadership. Magic Johnson and Phil Jackson knew that individual brilliance can only get you so far. It's about bringing people together, aligning them towards a common goal, and inspiring them to reach new heights. That's the kind of magic that truly transforms a team into a juggernaut.

But of course, let's not forget about handling pressure. Michael Jordan and the 2016 Cleveland Cavaliers showed us that when the stakes are high and the lights are brightest, that's when the real champions rise to the occasion. It's all about performing under stress, staying focused, and embracing the challenge. And then there's the lesson of learning from failure, as exemplified by Giannis Antetokounmpo and the San Antonio Spurs. These guys didn't let setbacks crush their spirit—they viewed them as opportunities to grow, to improve, and to come back even stronger. That's the power of the growth mindset, my friends.

Finally, we have the courage to break barriers, embodied by the trailblazing journeys of Jeremy Lin and Becky Hammon. They refused to be defined by society's limitations, daring to be different and making a positive impact in the process. Talk about inspiring the next generation, am I right?

"Okay, coach, these are all great lessons, but how do they all fit together?"

Well, my young ballers, the truth is, they're all interconnected. Success in basketball, and in life, often requires a combination of these attributes.

Resilience, for example, goes hand-in-hand with a growth mindset. The ability to bounce back from failure is fueled by the belief that you can always improve. And teamwork? Well, that's the foundation upon which you build all the other skills. No one achieves greatness alone.

I want you to keep every single one of these lessons close to your heart. Identify the areas in your life where you can apply them, whether it's on the basketball court, in the classroom, or in your personal relationships. And remember, growth and improvement are an ongoing process—there's always more to learn, more to achieve.

Now, I want to hear your thoughts. What resonated the most with you? What lessons do you plan to put into practice? And most importantly, how can you use these insights to make a positive impact, just like Jeremy Lin and Becky Hammon? Shoot me an honest review—I'm always eager to learn and improve. Together, we're going to keep pushing the boundaries of what's possible, one dribble, one shot, one triumph at a time.

REFERENCES

Ajit Nawalkha. (2017, March 13). *Why positive thinking builds courage, persistence, decisiveness (And 3 other AWESOME character traits)*. Medium; Medium. https://medium.com/@ajitna/why-positive-thinking-builds-courage-persistence-decisiveness-and-3-other-awesome-character-6ce16aff6f9a

Ameet Ranadive. (2016, March 25). *Fixed v. growth mindset*. Medium; Leadership. https://medium.com/leadership-motivation-and-impact/fixed-v-growth-mindset-902e7d0081b3

Aschburner, S. (2019, May 20). *Antetokounmpo learning how to deal with playoff disappointment*. Nba.com; NBA.com. https://www.nba.com/news/giannis-learning-bear-playoff-disappointment?experience=app

Augustyn, A. (2018). LeBron James American basketball player. In *Encyclopædia Britannica*. https://www.britannica.com/biography/LeBron-James

Augustyn, A. (2019a). Michael Jordan American basketball player. In *Encyclopædia Britannica*. https://www.britannica.com/biography/Michael-Jordan

Augustyn, A. (2019b). Stephen Curry American basketball player. In *Encyclopædia Britannica*. https://www.britannica.com/biography/Stephen-Curry

Augustyn, A. (2024a, August 23). *Cleveland Cavaliers American basketball team*. Encyclopedia Britannica. https://www.britannica.com/topic/Cleveland-Cavaliers

Augustyn, A. (2024b, August 31). *San Antonio Spurs American basketball team*. Encyclopedia Britannica. https://www.britannica.com/topic/San-Antonio-Spurs

Basketball mindset. (2022, March 24). Functionallawyer. https://www.functionallawyer.com/blog/basketball-mindset

basketballtrainer. (2023, September 27). *The role of psychology in basketball*. Basketball Trainer. https://basketballtrainer.com/role-of-psychology-in-basketball/

Becky Hammon Russian-American basketball player and coach. (2024). In *Encyclopædia Britannica*. https://www.britannica.com/biography/Becky-Harmon

Bhargava, Y. (2023, January 14). *"He makes his teammates better" - Magic Johnson reveals what are the traits that impress him the most about LeBron James.* Basketball Network - Your Daily Dose of Basketball. https://www.basketballnetwork.net/latest-news/magic-johnson-reveals-what-are-the-traits-that-impress-him-the-most-about-lebron-james

Biography.com Editors. (2014, April 3). *Derrick Rose.* Biography. https://www.biography.com/athlete/derrick-rose

Biography.com Editors, & Piccotti, T. (2021, August 31). *LeBron James.* Biography. https://www.biography.com/athletes/lebron-james

Boogaard, K. (2023, April 24). *You're already leading by example—here's how to make the most of that opportunity.* Getmarlee.com; Marlee. https://getmarlee.com/blog/leading-by-example

Brabeck, M., Jeffrey, J., & Fry, S. (2015). *Practice for knowledge acquisition (Not drill and kill).* American Psychological Association. https://www.apa.org/education-career/k12/practice-acquisition

Calhoun, L. G., Tedeschi, R. G., & Tedeschi, R. G. (1999). *Facilitating Posttraumatic Growth.* Routledge.

Cao, S., Geok, S. K., Roslan, S., Sun, H., Lam, S. K., & Qian, S. (2022). Mental fatigue and basketball performance: A systematic review. *Frontiers in Psychology, 12*(10.3389/fpsyg.2021.819081). https://doi.org/10.3389/fpsyg.2021.819081

Chamorro-Premuzic, T. (2022, May 25). *How to deal with high-pressure situations at work.* Harvard Business Review. https://hbr.org/2022/05/how-to-deal-with-high-pressure-situations-at-work

Chan, K. (2023, June 16). *5 Types of adversity and ways to overcome them.* Verywell Mind. https://www.verywellmind.com/types-of-adversity-and-ways-to-overcome-them-7505840

Charania, S. (2018, October 31). "They just don't know me": Derrick Rose opens up about overcoming injuries and adversity to revive his career. *The New York Times.* https://www.nytimes.com/athletic/622474/2018/10/31/they-just-dont-know-me-derrick-rose-opens-up-about-overcoming-injuries-and-adversity-to-revive-his-career/

Coffey, D. (2012, September 4). *Basketball psychology: How mental attitudes shape performance.* Sports Psychology Today. https://www.sportpsychologytoday.com/youth-sports-psychology/how-mental-attitudes-shape-performance/

Deng, P. (2020, June 20). *What basketball taught me about life.* Medium. https://pachdeng.medium.com/what-basketball-taught-me-about-life-10491e66ac0c

Dresie, L. (2024, June 15). *Ten years ago, the Spurs achieved ultimate redemption against the Heat.* Pounding the Rock; Pounding The Rock. https://www.poundingtherock.com/2024/6/15/24178379/ten-years-ago-the-spurs-achieved-ultimate-redemption-against-the-heat

Dunn, B. (2024, March 5). *Beyond the court: Life lessons from 30 years of coaching basketball.* The Center Consulting Group. https://www.centerconsulting.org/blog/beyond-the-court-life-lessons-from-30-years-of-coaching-basketball

Dweck, C. (2016). *What having a "Growth Mindset" actually mean.* Harvard Business Review. https://hbr.org/2016/01/what-having-a-growth-mindset-actually-means

Edmondson, A. (2011, April). *Strategies for learning from failure.* Harvard Business Review. https://hbr.org/2011/04/strategies-for-learning-from-failure

8 Valuable life lessons kids learn from playing basketball. (2018, June 14). Toronto Athletic Camps. https://tacsports.ca/8-valuable-life-lessons-kids-learn-playing-basketball/

Flakes, K. (2020, March 3). *11 Tips for applying Kobe Bryant's Mamba Mentality to your career.* Medium; Kenneth Flakes Professional Plus. https://medium.com/professional-plus/11-tips-for-applying-kobe-bryants-mamba-mentality-to-your-career-4e90a544a1a6

From underrated to undeniable. (2022, July 4). NBA.com. https://www.nba.com/warriors/news/from-underrated-to-undeniable-20230727

Gadirajurrett, H., Srinivasan, R., Stevens, J., & Jeena, N. (2018). *Impact of leadership on team's performance impact of leadership on team's performance.* https://pdxscholar.library.pdx.edu/cgi/viewcontent.cgi?article=2911&context=etm_studentprojects#:~:text=Leaders

Gasparinetti, F. (2023, June 16). *Discover how consistency and dedication can help you build strong habits and achieve your goals. Learn effective strategies and practical.* LinkedIn. https://www.linkedin.com/pulse/key-building-strong-habits-consistency-dedication-gasparinetti

Gibson, D. K. (2021, October 20). *Jeremy Lin on racism, mental health, and the problem with game highlights.* The Aspen Institute. https://www.aspeninstitute.org/blog-posts/jeremy-lin-on-racism-mental-health-and-the-problem-with-game-highlights/

Hansford, C. (2023, June 6). *Lakers news: Magic Johnson explains how his leadership style is similar to heat's Jimmy Butler*. Lakers Nation. https://lakersnation.com/lakers-news-magic-johnson-explains-how-his-leadership-style-is-similar-to-heats-jimmy-butler/#:~:text=Magic%20was%20not%20only%20one

Honaker, K. (2020, April 22). *Michael Jordan's most clutch moments in his career*. ClutchPoints. https://clutchpoints.com/michael-jordans-most-clutch-moments

Hurley, K. (2024, February 17). *What is resilience? Definition, types, building resiliency, benefits, and resources*. Everyday Health. https://www.everydayhealth.com/wellness/resilience/

IanSanders. (2017, October 10). *Having the courage to be different when everyone around you screams "fit in!"* Medium. https://iansanders.medium.com/having-the-courage-to-be-different-when-everyone-arounds-you-screams-fit-in-946fa255cb5a

Jenkins, K. (2024, June 13). *What are the biggest comebacks in NBA Finals history?* ESPN; ESPN. https://www.espn.com/nba/story/_/id/40337606/what-biggest-comebacks-nba-finals-history#:~:text=The%20Cleveland%20Cavaliers

Jeremy Lin stats. (2010). Basketball Reference. https://www.basketball-reference.com/players/l/linje01.html

Kamaldeen Kehinde. (2019, December 27). *How to break barriers without guidance*. Medium; Medium. https://medium.com/@devyousefk/how-to-break-barriers-without-guidance-a3908d2451f1

Khan, S. (2024, May 4). *7 Lessons from basketball that elevated me to success*. Medium; ILLUMINATION. https://medium.com/illumination/7-lessons-from-basketball-that-elevated-me-to-success-229e7d2d15e6

Klinzing, M. (2015, April 4). *Basketball on the edge - How basketball can lead to a lifetime of success*. Head Start Basketball Camps. https://headstartbasketball.com/basketball-on-the-edge-how-basketball-can-lead-to-a-lifetime-of-success/

Kobe Bryant facts and related content. (n.d.). Encyclopedia Britannica. https://www.britannica.com/facts/Kobe-Bryant

Lawrence, A. (2023, July 19). Stephen Curry is too good to pretend his success is merely down to hard work. *The Guardian*. https://www.theguardian.com/sport/2023/jul/19/stephen-curry-documentary-movie-apple-tv-review

Leung, M. (2013). Jeremy Lin's Model Minority Problem. *Contexts, 12*(3), 52–56. https://doi.org/10.1177/1536504213499879

Logan, R. G. (2019). Phil Jackson American basketball player and coach. In *Encyclopædia Britannica*. https://www.britannica.com/biography/Phil-Jackson

Long, J. (2016, April 27). *The importance of practice – And our reluctance to do it.* Harvard Business Publishing. https://www.harvardbusiness.org/the-importance-of-practice-and-our-reluctance-to-do-it/

McMenamin, D. (2020, December 31). *Spurs' Hammon 1st woman to direct NBA team.* ESPN. https://www.espn.com/nba/story/_/id/30627408/spurs-becky-hammon-becomes-first-woman-nba-regular-season-history-act-head-coach

Medarametla, A. (2021, February 12). *Lebron James' rise.* The Observer. https://observer.case.edu/lebron-james-rise/

Middleton, T. (2024, January 25). *The importance of teamwork (as proven by science).* Work Life; Atlassian. https://www.atlassian.com/blog/teamwork/the-importance-of-teamwork

Mike. (2023, June 19). *Basketball: How the sport prepares you for life.* LuHi Summer Programs. https://luhisummercamps.org/basketball-how-the-sport-prepares-you-for-life/

Natian, J. (2023, March 21). *I followed Kobe Bryant's daily routine for a week (training, basketball, diet, Mamba Mentality).* Medium; Medium. https://medium.com/@natian1229/i-followed-kobe-bryants-daily-routine-for-a-week-training-basketball-diet-mamba-mentality-5dc4cd006de9

Perry, E. (2022, January 31). *10 Ways to overcome adversity and thrive during hard times.* BetterUp. https://www.betterup.com/blog/how-to-overcome-adversity

Phil Jackson: Zen master's guide to basketball success. (2024, April 13). Basketball. https://www.coachstat.net/phil-jackson-the-zen-master#:~:text=Phil%20Jackson

Raab, C. (2023, February 3). *Courage: The vital aspect of sustainability leadership we don't talk about enough.* Trellis; Trellis. https://trellis.net/article/courage-vital-aspect-sustainability-leadership-we-dont-talk-about-enough/

Reynolds, T. (2023, February 3). *LeBron James' off-court legacy complements NBA success.* NBA.com. https://www.nba.com/news/lebron-james-off-court-legacy-complements-nba-success

San Antonio Spurs scores, stats, and highlights. (n.d.). ESPN. https://www.espn.com/nba/team/_/name/sa/san-antonio-spurs

Sardin, J. (2023, April 23). *What are the biggest challenges faced by basketball players throughout their careers? - Sport Combine.* Sport Combine. https://sport-combine.com/en/blog/what-are-the-biggest-challenges-faced-by-basketball-players-throughout-their-careers/

Scott, E. (2022, September 26). *How to stop putting pressure on yourself.* Verywell Mind. https://www.verywellmind.com/how-to-stop-putting-pressure-on-yourself-3144724

Sharma, S. (2019, June 18). *Phil Jackson the Zen master who conquered basketball.* Medium. https://sunilsharmauk.medium.com/phil-jackson-the-zen-master-who-conquered-basketball-e8257a76979d

Shelburne, R. (2014, June 16). *NBA playoffs: San Antonio Spurs rise from 2013 NBA Finals loss.* ESPN; ESPN. https://www.espn.com/nba/playoffs/2014/story/_/id/11092092/san-antonio-spurs-rise-2013-nba-finals-loss

Sima, A. (2015, September 15). *Breaking Barriers: Overcoming obstacles to achieve happiness & success.* LinkedIn. https://www.linkedin.com/pulse/breaking-barriers-overcoming-obstacles-achieve-happiness-allison-sima/

Sirk, C. (2019, November 29). *Zen and the art of winning: Phil Jackson's team leadership.* CRM.org. https://crm.org/articles/zen-and-the-art-of-winning-phil-jacksons-team-leadership

Smith, J. A. (2022). *How to learn from your failures.* Greater Good. https://greatergood.berkeley.edu/article/item/how_to_learn_from_your_failures#thank-influence

Smith, L., & Smith, L. (2019, June 18). *Believe in yourself: Tips for breaking barriers and following your dreams.* Linda's Life. https://lindaslife.com/believe-in-yourself-tips-for-breaking-barriers-and-following-your-dreams/

Stress. (2023). World Health Organization. https://www.who.int//news-room/questions-and-answers/item/stress/?gad_source=1&gclid=CjwKCAjw_4S3BhAAEiwA_64YhkYk-O6iY8aAxlMSsLRBbIxHpMmItSH4kNrm1s0Ta34oKx8b83AxIBoCJ7UQAvD_BwE

Tafuri, G. (2023, July 26). *Sports psychology: The role of mental toughness in basketball success.* Dunkest NBA. https://www.dunkest.com/en/nba/news/146927/sports-psychology-the-role-of-mental-toughness-in-basketball-success

Teamwork and leadership. (2019). Github. https://saylordotorg.github.io/text_business-communication-for-success/s23-05-teamwork-and-leadership.html

10 Proven ways on how to overcome adversity in life. (n.d.). Tonyrobbins.com. https://www.tonyrobbins.com/blog/overcoming-adversity

The art of staying focused under pressure. (2020, June 3). Criteria for Success. https://criteriaforsuccess.com/the-art-of-staying-focused-under-pressure/#:~:text=Focus%20on%20one%20thing%20at%20the%20time&text=This%20way%2C%20you%20allow%20yourself

The benefits of kids playing basketball at a young age. (n.d.). Spalding. https://www.spalding.com.au/blog/the-benefits-of-kids-playing-basketball-at-a-young-age

The curious case of Derrick Rose's injuries. (2022, January 17). Silverman Ankle & Foot - Edina Orthopedic Surgeon. https://www.anklefootmd.com/the-curious-case-of-derrick-roses-injuries/

The Editors of Encyclopedia Britannica. (2019). Magic Johnson American basketball player. In *Encyclopædia Britannica*. https://www.britannica.com/biography/Magic-Johnson

The mental game of basketball: Strategies for overcoming challenges. (2024, September 9). On the Court. https://onthecourt.us/blog/the-mental-game-of-basketball-strategies-for-overcoming-challenges

The power of consistency: How to achieve success through discipline and dedication. (2023, May 15). Enduralab. https://www.enduralab.com/blog/the-power-of-consistency-how-to-achieve-success-through-discipline-and-dedication

Tikkanen, A. (2023, November 9). *Giannis Antetokounmpo Greek basketball player*. Encyclopedia Britannica. https://www.britannica.com/biography/Giannis-Antetokounmpo

Top 10 clutch performances in basketball history. (2016). Marygrove College Athletics. https://www.marygrovemustangs.com/top-10-clutch-performances-in-basketball-history.html

2016 NBA Finals. (2021, October 19). Wikipedia. https://en.wikipedia.org/wiki/2016_NBA_Finals

2016 Sounds of the finals: Cavs complete historic comeback. (2024). NBA.com. https://www.nba.com/watch/video/2016-sounds-of-the-finals?plsrc=nba&collection=best-of-cavaliers-warriors-rivalry

UMAIR, M. (2020, May 5). *Importance of teamwork in leadership.* Medium. https://medium.com/@imumair.mech/importance-of-teamwork-in-leadership-42570c9560c9

Voltage Control. (2024, July). *Successful collaborative leadership in action: Case studies and real-world examples.* Voltage Control. https://voltagecontrol.com/articles/successful-collaborative-leadership-in-action-case-studies-and-real-world-examples/

Warrell, D. M. (2023, December 19). *Failing is hard, but not near as hard as learning from It.* Forbes. https://www.forbes.com/sites/margiewarrell/2023/12/19/think-failure-is-hard-try-learning-from-it/

Wikipedia Contributors. (2019, September 17). *Jeremy Lin.* Wikipedia; Wikimedia Foundation. https://en.wikipedia.org/wiki/Jeremy_Lin

Wikipedia Contributors. (2024, September 6). *Becky Hammon.* Wikipedia; Wikimedia Foundation. https://en.wikipedia.org/wiki/Becky_Hammon#:~:text=On%20December%2030%2C%202020%2C%20Hammon

Yam, K. (2022, February 16). *Jeremy Lin reflects on "Linsanity" 10 years later, gets candid about "big regret."* NBC News. https://www.nbcnews.com/news/asian-america/jeremy-lin-reflects-linsanity-10-years-later-gets-candid-big-regret-rcna15364

Yue, A. L. S. (2020, July 18). *What competitive sports taught me about resilience and mental toughness.* Medium. https://alexlohsengyue.medium.com/what-competitive-sports-taught-me-about-resilience-and-mental-toughness-31a99eb8208e

Zhou, Y., & Zhou, F. (2019). Cognitive neural mechanism of sports competition pressure source. *Translational Neuroscience, 10*(1), 147–151. https://doi.org/10.1515/tnsci-2019-0025

Image References

Freepik. (2024). *All images supplied by Freepik - Free Graphic resources for everyone.* Freepik. https://www.freepik.com/

Made in the USA
Las Vegas, NV
18 December 2024

14633542R00075